Contents

access to history

in depth

DISORDER *and* REBELLION *in* TUDOR ENGLAND

Nicholas Fellows

HODDER
EDUCATION
AN HACHETTE UK COMPANY

Acknowledgements

The front cover illustration shows 'The Family of Henry VIII: An Allegory of the Tudor Succession' by Lucas de Heere, reproduced courtesy of The National Museum of Wales.

The publishers would like to thank the following individuals, institutions and companies for permission to reproduce copyright illustrations in this book:

The Baroness Herries, page 34; The British Library, page 91; The National Portrait Gallery, pages 73 and 83; Victoria & Albert Museum, London, UK/Bridgeman Art Library, page 29.

Every effort has been made to trace and acknowledge ownership of copyright. The publishers will be glad to make arrangements with any copyright holders whom it has not been able to contact.

Order:Please contact Bookpoint Ltd, 130 Milton Park, Abingdon, Oxon OX14 4SB. Telephone: (44) 01235 827720. Fax: (44) 01235 400454. Lines are open from 9am - 5pm Monday to Saturday, with a 24-hour message answering service. You can also order through our website at www.hoddereducation.co.uk

British Library Cataloguing in Publication Data
A catalogue record for this title is available from the British Library

ISBN-13: 978 0 340 78143 2

First published 2001
Impression number   10 9 8
Year   2009

Copyright © 2001 Nick Fellows

Typeset by Fakenham Photosetting Ltd, Fakenham, Norfolk.
Printed in Great Britain for Hodder Murray, an imprint of Hodder Education, a member of the Hodder Headline Group, an Hachette UK Company, 338 Euston Road, London NW1 3BH by CPI Antony Rowe

Preface

The original *Access to History* series was conceived as a collection of sets of books covering popular chronological periods in British history, together with the histories of other countries, such as France, Germany, Russia and the USA. This arrangement complemented the way in which history has traditionally been taught in sixth forms, colleges and universities. In recent years, however, other ways of dividing up the past have become increasingly popular. In particular, there has been a greater emphasis on studying relatively brief periods in considerable detail and on comparing similar historical phenomena in different countries. These developments have generated a demand for appropriate learning materials, and, in response, two new 'strands' have been added to the main series – *In Depth* and *Themes*. The new volumes build directly on the features that have made *Access to History* so popular.

To the General Reader

Access books have been specifically designed to meet the needs of examination students, but they also have much to offer the general reader. The authors are committed to the belief that good history must not only be accurate, up-to-date and scholarly, but also clearly and attractively written. The main body of the text (excluding the Study Guide sections) should therefore form a readable and engaging survey of a topic. Moreover, each author has aimed not merely to provide as clear an explanation as possible of what happened in the past but also to stimulate readers and to challenge them into thinking for themselves about the past and its significance. Thus, although no prior knowledge is expected from the reader, he or she is treated as an intelligent and thinking person throughout. The author tends to share ideas and explore possibilities, instead of delivering so-called 'historical truths' from on high.

To the student reader

It is intended that *Access* books should be used by students studying history at a higher level. Its volumes are all designed to be working texts, which should be reasonably clear on a first reading but which will benefit from re-reading and close study.

To be an effective and successful student, you need to budget your time wisely. Hence you should think carefully about how important the material in a particular book is for you. If you simply need to acquire a general grasp of a topic, the following approach will probably be effective:

1. Read Chapter 1, which should give you an overview of the whole book, and think about its contents.

2. Skim through Chapter 2, paying particular attention to the 'Points to Consider' box and to the 'Key Issue' highlighted at the start of each section. Decide if you need to read the whole chapter.
3. If you do, read the chapter, stopping at the end of every sub-division of the text to make notes.
4. Repeat stage 2 (and stage 3 where appropriate) for the other chapters.

If, however, your course demands a detailed knowledge of the contents of the book, you will need to be correspondingly more thorough. There is no perfect way of studying, and it is particularly worthwhile experimenting with different styles of note-making to find the one that best suits you. Nevertheless the following plan of action is worth trying:

1. Read a whole chapter quickly, preferably at one sitting. Avoid the temptation – which may be very great – to make notes at this stage.
2. Study the diagram at the end of the chapter, ensuring that you understand the general 'shape' of what you have read.
3. Re-read the chapter more slowly, this time taking notes. You may well be amazed at how much more intelligible and straightforward the material seems on a second reading – and your notes will be correspondingly more useful to you when you have to write an essay or revise for an exam. In the long run, reading a chapter twice can, in fact, often save time. Be sure to make your notes in a clear, orderly fashion, and spread them out so that, if necessary, you can later add extra information.
4. The Study Guide sections will be particularly valuable for those taking AS Level, A Level and Higher. Read the advice on essay questions, and do tackle the specimen titles. (Remember that if learning is to be effective, it must be active. No one – alas – has yet devised any substitute for real effort. It is up to you to make up your own mind on the key issues in any topic.)
5. Attempt the *Source-based questions* section. The guidance on tackling these exercises is well worth reading and thinking about.

When you have finished the main chapters, go through the 'Further Reading' section. Remember that no single book can ever do more than introduce a topic, and it is to be hoped that, time permitting, you will want to read more widely. If *Access* books help you to discover just how diverse and fascinating the human past can be, the series will have succeeded in its aim – and you will experience that enthusiasm for the subject which, along with efficient learning, is the hallmark of the best students.

Robert Pearce

1 Introduction

POINTS TO CONSIDER

This chapter places Tudor rebellions in the wider context of unrest in the Medieval and Early Modern period. It will then go on to look at the legacy of the Wars of the Roses, before examining the forces available to uphold royal authority. Your aim will be to consider whether the Tudor period should be seen as one of disquiet and unrest or a period of relative stability. You should keep these points in mind and be prepared to modify your views as you study the rebellions in greater depth.

KEY DATES

1348	The Black Death
1381	The Peasants' Revolt
1450	Cade's Rebellion
1455–85	The Wars of the Roses
1485	Battle of Bosworth
1536	Pilgrimage of Grace
1549	Ket's Rebellion
1569	Northern Rising
1596	Oxfordshire rising
1601	Essex Rebellion
1607	Midland Revolt
1642	Civil War
1685	Monmouth Rebellion, Argyll rebellion

1 Tudor Rebellions in Context

KEY ISSUE Was the Tudor period a time of unrest?

Looking back today, our picture of the sixteenth century is of the long and secure reigns of Henry VIII and Elizabeth I. According to this view, the Tudor period brought stability and peace after the turmoil of the fifteenth century. Our early memories from school history of the Tudors reinforce this interpretation with the Holbein portrait of Henry VIII or Hilliard's of Elizabeth. Although Henry VII had won the crown on the battlefield at Bosworth in 1485 he secured the throne and passed it on safely to his son and his children. It is almost as if the triumph of the Tudors was guaranteed. However, this tells only half the story, as the sixteenth century witnessed a large number of rebellions, some of which came very close to overthrowing the monarchy.

Within a year of defeating Richard III, Henry VII was faced by the challenge of the pretender Lambert Simnel. To contemporaries it must have appeared that Bosworth had failed to settle anything. The greatest challenges to the regime were in 1540–1563 when there were a series of disastrous foreign wars, four attempted coups, three serious rebellions, the rule of an ageing bully, followed by a young boy and then a woman, as well as a female usurper. If this was not enough, there were a series of epidemics and of economic and financial catastrophes. Furthermore, more than half a century later Elizabeth was still facing challenges with the Oxfordshire rising of 1596 and the Essex rebellion of 1601. The Tudor regime faced challenges throughout the fifteenth and sixteenth centuries and although law, order and legitimacy would triumph in the end, it was a close-run thing.

Although historians tend to study their period in isolation, Tudor rebellions need to be seen in the wider context of the late Medieval and Early Modern periods. The three centuries from 1381 to 1685 witnessed recurrent regional uprisings, not to mention a large number of village revolts. Unrest soon followed the Black Death of 1348, and may be linked to its consequences. The reduction in the population of England by one-third meant that the peasantry was in a much stronger position: the size of the workforce had declined and those left could demand higher wages and improved conditions. As a result, the feudal ties that had helped to keep the peasantry under control were substantially loosened as the nobility had less authority over the lives of the peasants.

Were the Tudor rebellions anything more than a continuation of the unrest that had started with the Peasants' Revolt of 1381? The disturbances had continued with Cade's rising of 1450 and appeared to reach a climax with the Wars of the Roses in the second half of the fifteenth century. The scale of events, such as the Pilgrimage of Grace in 1536 and Ket's rising of 1549, was similar to many of the disturbances of the Wars of the Roses, suggesting that unrest and lawlessness were still major issues. Religious changes and confusion in the mid-sixteenth century had not helped, as the Reformation undermined much of the traditional authority of the church and further reduced the influence of another instrument of social control. Although the number and size of the rebellions facing the Tudors declined after the Northern Rising of 1569, unrest did not end then. Disturbances continued under the Stuarts with the Midland Rising of 1607, the Civil Wars of the 1640s and the Monmouth and Argyll rebellions of 1685.

2 The Legacy of the Wars of the Roses

KEY ISSUE What was the legacy of the Wars of the Roses?

The issue of the succession to the English throne had been a major problem from 1399, when the nobility, disillusioned with the weak and arbitrary rule of Richard II, had replaced him with Henry Bolingbroke. Although stability returned under Henry and his son Henry V, this did not last. The death of Henry V in 1422 left England ruled by a minor, Henry VI. However, it was only when Henry VI reached adulthood that serious problems began. Henry VI was unable to maintain control of the nobility, and another claimant, Richard of York, emerged. As a result, the 1450s saw a continual struggle between the Yorkists and Lancastrians for the crown. This culminated in 1461 when Edward, Duke of York, the son of Richard, was able to defeat Henry VI and seize the crown. However, the stability Edward brought did not last as he died in 1483 leaving his 12-year-old son as heir. Once again the succession was thrown into confusion as Edward's brother, Richard, seized the throne.

The continual upheavals, large-scale battles and frequent changes to the succession throughout the fifteenth century created instability and suggested that military might, rather than legitimacy, was the main factor in determining who should rule. As a consequence the nobility became accustomed to fighting to determine who would rule. The legacy of this was to last well into the sixteenth century as many Tudor rebellions were concerned with the succession question.

A further consequence of the unrest and weak royal authority was the growth of private armies. In order to protect themselves and to take advantage of the chaos many of the nobles created their own armed forces. When the nobility felt threatened, or if they wanted to impose their own will, they were able to call upon this force to resolve disputes. This encouraged those with large forces to intimidate and threaten others, even the king, and resulted in a decline in respect for law and order. The nobles used their armies to intimidate juries and to threaten, or even overturn, royal will. The emergence of 'over-mighty subjects' meant that there were areas where the royal writ did not run. Here magnates were accustomed to having their own way.

However, despite the turmoil of the Wars of the Roses most of the population wanted a quiet life. Christine Carpenter has convincingly argued that it took real provocation before the nobility was willing to resort to disorder. The propertied class had the most to lose from unrest. Therefore it is important to realise that the Wars of the Roses started only when all attempts to find a peaceful solution to the problems of kingship had been exhausted. Order had only collapsed because the government had not carried out their traditional duties of rendering justice and resolving disputes. England was not a naturally unruly land, but the unrest that characterised the fifteenth century may have made it harder for monarchs to reassert control in the sixteenth. On the other hand, it can also be argued that the anarchy of the Wars of the Roses had a more positive influence: many in society became determined to avoid a return to chaos and disorder.

3 The Forces of Authority

> **KEY ISSUE** What forces were available to the monarch to keep order?

a) Formal authority

Although there are times today when governments are threatened by disorder and riots, they have a police force, judicial system and, in times of an emergency, the armed forces to call upon. This was not the situation in early modern England. The king had no police force, and at local level had to rely upon the unpaid services of the nobility and gentry to act as Lord Lieutenants, Sheriffs or Justices of the Peace (JPs). These men were not trained in preserving the peace. They probably participated in local government because it brought them prestige and status among their peers. However, the king depended upon their upholding the law and putting into practice his wishes. If they did not, his position and authority were undermined.

The king did not have a regular, professional army available. He lacked the financial means to maintain such a force (which, if it had existed, would have been seen as a threat to the liberties of the people). After the Wars of the Roses Henry VII passed laws to prevent the nobility keeping private armies that could be used to defy the law and intimidate JPs. However, this also removed a potential force that could be used to maintain order in the localities. The virtual ending of this feudal system resulted in the decline of the 'feudal host' as a means of levying troops. As a result the monarch had to develop and build up a relationship with the localities whereby local nobles and gentry could be relied upon to maintain order and at least buy the monarch time so that he himself could assemble a force to deal with unrest. If this relationship between central government and the localities broke down, then order might soon collapse.

The monarch had a variety of ways of trying to ensure that his will and laws were accepted. Although the Tudors did not fully develop the concept of the Divine Right of Kings, the idea that they were appointed by God helped to create a certain amount of mystique and respect. God had given sovereigns to the realm and expected them to be obeyed.[1] Although it was difficult for Henry VII to claim divine appointment, as he owed his throne to victory on the battlefield, even claimed that he was 'Henry, by the grace of God, King'. This concept also had less impact when the country was ruled by a Protector or Lord President. There were other ways for monarchs to show their power. Henry VIII was able to do this on the battlefield, where his military prowess prompted parallels with the successful warrior Henry V. This was much harder for a minor or a female ruler, but it did not stop Elizabeth rallying the troops at Tilbury before the Armada. Monarchs could also show themselves to their people by progresses through the kingdom. Although their travels did not usually take them beyond the south and home counties it must have strongly impressed those who watched the monarch and his entourage. Tudor monarchs also built a large number of palaces. They were large and decorated with symbols of the Tudors: a clear sign to all who saw them from the fields, or who stayed in them, of the might of the monarchy. Within the palaces paintings and portraits were used to add to the image of power and authority. However, these were seen by very few. But monarchs were still able to convey the royal image to their subjects. Coins, even the lower denominations, carried pictures of the monarch, and from the middle of Henry VIII's reign a greater effort was made to portray their power. Their importance is shown most clearly in Edward's reign. The numerous issues show a progression in imagery designed for maximum political impact. The first coins show a young boy, later coins show Edward crowned and holding the symbols of state, whilst the last coins show him mounted on horseback, ready to take on his military role. The coins were the strongest way of promoting the monarch as they were available to nearly everyone.

However, there were times when imagery was not enough and subjects had to be told directly what was expected. The first way for the king's authority to reach the masses quickly was by royal proclamations. They were used to tell the population the orders of the monarch and to remind them of their obedience during times of crisis. Their form was designed to impress and they were sealed with the Great Seal. Messengers were sent out to carry them around the country, where they were to be published in churches, or read out by local officials. Although not everyone would see a proclamation, word soon spread and the monarchs could make their will known to a good number of people.

The church also acted as a bedrock of authority. It had been a source of authority in late-medieval society, its rituals enforced discipline and it preached a moral order. On the whole the clergy were respected and their moral authority gave them a great deal of influence. The church was also an effective means of reaching the population as a whole. Preaching could be used to inform people of royal policy in all the 9,500 parishes, and as everyone was expected to attend church every week this provided a quick and easy way to reach large numbers. However, the changes of the Reformation weakened the role of the church and the priest lost some of his special status. As a result, not all priests were willing to uphold royal policy in their sermons. In order to overcome this, the Edwardian government issued Homilies, or printed sermons, to be read in all churches. Many of them taught that all authority came from royal power. The Reformation also meant that some parishioners did not attend church because they did not agree with the new doctrine, whilst others preferred the alehouse or sleep. But even if they did attend there was still no guarantee that they listened to what they were told. However, it is likely that over time the message of obedience did sink in. By the end of the Tudor period the church was teaching national loyalty as much as Christian faith.[2]

There was still one ultimate weapon left to the monarch: death. Throughout the period Tudor monarchs used the Treason laws to reinforce authority. This was a particularly valuable weapon after the Reformation, when it was used to enforce support for Henry's marriage to Anne Boleyn and to remove those who opposed the break with Rome. Very often its selective use acted as a warning to others, encouraging them to obey the wishes of the monarch. It was especially useful after a rebellion, when ringleaders, especially among the lower orders, could be almost certain of death.

b) Informal authority

There were also a number of indirect ways in which law and order was reinforced. The first of these was through the hierarchical structure of the family. This was a particularly useful method as it operated and was reinforced every day. The head of the household was to be obeyed and any who resisted made to conform. This authority was reinforced by the church. It taught that obedience to the head of the household was required by God. With the decline in respect for the priest after the Reformation the head of the household took on an even greater significance in reinforcing the idea of obedience to authority.

The family was perceived as a microcosm of the state where the husband, or father, was the equivalent of the monarch and had power over his wife, children and servants. The system taught that everyone was expected to obey their superiors. This belief connected the theory of obligation and obedience with the doctrine of the Great Chain of Being and was well explained by Sir John Fortescue, writing in the fifteenth century:

1   God created as many different kinds of things as he did creatures, so that there is no creature which does not differ in some respect superior or inferior to all the rest. So that from the highest angel down to the lowest of his kind there is absolutely not found an angel that has not a superior or
5   inferior; nor from man down to the meanest worm is there any creature which is not in some respect superior to one creature and inferior to another. So that there is nothing which the bond of order does not embrace.

This idea was commonplace in Tudor England and reinforced the belief in an unfaltering order. It also taught that the themes of loyalty and obligation applied downwards as well as upwards. Those at the top of the chain had duties and responsibilities, just like those at the bottom. However, this belief in a society of orders, where all had their place and role, did not always help in the preservation of peace. Instead, at times of unrest, it encouraged the lower orders to look to their superiors among the gentry and nobility for leadership. When this happened and the gentry joined the commons, it was often a sign that they shared their belief that the government was showing contempt for the society of orders. It also ensured that the rising became a serious problem as the gentlemen failed to perform their expected task of keeping order in the localities.

4 Conclusion

> **KEY ISSUE** How rebellion-prone were the Tudors?

The apparently large number of rebellions that provides the substance for this book suggests that both formal and informal authority failed to uphold order. However, although every Tudor monarch faced challenges from some of their subjects, it must be stressed that many of the rebellions you will study were against the perceived enemies of the state, not the state itself. Frequently the rioters believed that they were upholding the social order. As this introduction has shown, the channels of authority available to the state were limited, but they were remarkably successful. Most of the population obeyed authority at both a national and local level. The population was always reluctant to support causes that they felt lacked legitimacy. Over the whole Tudor period, from a total population of some 15 million who reached adulthood, probably no more than 65,000 actively rebelled, and most of them were in the Pilgrimage of Grace. As you read the rest of the book remember that the people were not prone to violent rebellion: it was usually the last desperate act when all other attempts to redress their grievance had failed.

References

1 Alison Wall, *Power and Protest in England 1525–1640* (Arnold, 2000), p. 12.
2 Wall, *Power and Protest*, p. 13.

Summary Diagram
Introduction: Rebellion in Context

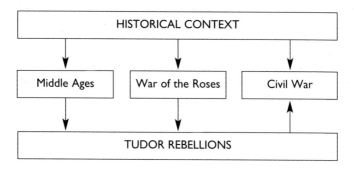

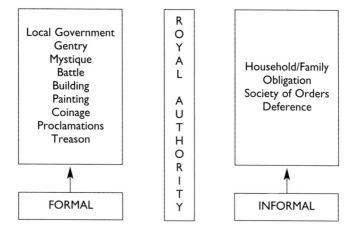

Working on Chapter I

You will need to make notes as you read this book. They will help to consolidate your ideas and organise your thoughts, as well as being the basis for both your essay writing and revision. Make sure that you break up your notes, use headings and sub-headings, buy a variety of coloured pens so that you can underline in different colours. You will soon discover that it is easier to revise from a page of well set out notes than it is from a page of solid writing. The headings and sub-divisions in the book should help you make a start. The way that you set out your notes will depend upon personal preference, but make sure that you do not finish up copying out the book! There are a variety of ways to organise your notes – by lists, spider or line diagrams or charts. Find a way that suits you and stick to it.

At this stage it is also a good idea to make sure you are fully aware of the syllabus or specification that you are studying as this will have an important impact on your approach to the topic. You need to know whether you are studying some, or all, the rebellions as part of an outline paper or as a theme covering the whole century. If it is the latter the last chapter will be particularly important for you as you will need to be comparing the rebellions, looking for similarities and differences.

2 Securing the dynasty: The reign of Henry VII

POINTS TO CONSIDER

This chapter examines Henry VII's inheritance and the legacy of the Wars of the Roses before going on to consider his claim to the throne and the threat posed by the nobility. It concludes with an examination of the major challenges to his rule. You will need to consider how serious these challenges were and what they reveal about the power of the English monarchy.

KEY DATES

1483	The Usurpation of Richard III. The Buckingham Rebellion suggests that there is support for Henry Tudor.
1485	Battle of Bosworth. Richard III defeated, Henry Tudor becomes king.
1486	Rebellion of Lord Lovell.
1486–7	Simnel Rebellion. He receives support from Ireland, Burgundy and Lovell. Defeated at the Battle of Stoke.
1489	Yorkshire taxation rebellion.
1491–9	Warbeck rebellion. He receives support from Ireland, France, Burgundy, Scotland and the Stanleys.
1499	Cornish taxation rebellion. Rebels reach Blackheath before being defeated.
1499–1506	Rebellion of the Duke of Suffolk.

1 The Battle of Bosworth

> **KEY ISSUE** Was Bosworth a successful Tudor Rebellion?

The Wars of the Roses had divided the political nation, creating two sides, as factionalism at court had spilled over into conflict in the countryside. As a consequence those who were out of favour were always likely to offer their support to anyone who might restore their political fortune. Conflict had been a way of life for many in the second half of the fifteenth century and settling the succession by force was not new. It is against this background that we need to consider the challenge of Henry Tudor.

Henry Tudor was never going to inherit the throne through birth. His claim to the throne of England was very weak. It was through his mother, Margaret Beaufort, who was a direct descendant of Edward III, through the marriage of his third son, John of Gaunt. However, John's children had been born before he was married and an act of parliament had actually excluded them from the throne. Henry himself was an obscure Lancastrian, who was scarcely known in England. If he was to become king it would have to be through force, and there were many who believed he would not keep the throne, even if he were able to win it. However, his chances of gaining the throne were given an enormous boost by the usurpation of Richard III in 1483. The seizure of the throne changed the political climate in England. By usurping the throne and denying the succession of Edward V, Richard had laid himself open to challenge. The disappearance of Edward's young sons was suspicious and alienated many, including Edward IV's widow, who would now look to transfer their support to other claimants. Plots to remove Richard soon surfaced as those dissatisfied with his rule looked to replace him. Henry also shrewdly drew up plans to marry Edward IV's daughter, helping him to gain support from both Yorkists and Lancastrians. Signs of dissatisfaction with Richard were soon evident as Richard's former ally, the Duke of Buckingham, turned against him and led a rising in favour of Henry in October 1483. However, this was too soon and Henry, having initially set sail for England, wisely turned back to Brittany. He was joined in exile by men such as the Earl of Oxford, Edward Poynings, John Morton and Richard Fox. They gave him a base of support, though without foreign assistance he would stand little chance.

As Henry was to discover later, foreign aid was crucial in turning a rising into something more meaningful. He was fortunate in that the King of France was willing to provide financial help and Henry was able to sail for England in August 1485 with an army of some 500 loyal exiles and about 1,500 second-rate French troops. The expedition landed in Wales, where Henry hoped to use his ancestral links to win much needed further support. He was able to win over influential men such as Rhys ap Thomas, with the promise of reward should Richard be defeated. However, it was the support of the higher nobility that he really needed. He had hoped to get support from the Stanleys, but this was not immediately forthcoming because Richard held Lord Stanley's eldest son hostage and others were not willing to gamble their political careers until they were certain of the outcome.

As Henry made his way further into central England, Richard realised that he would have to face him in battle. The two armies met on 22nd August near Market Bosworth. Henry's army numbered 3,000, but Richard's nearer 5,000. The battle was fierce with heavy casualties, but the turning point came when Richard gambled by trying to strike directly at Henry. At this point the Stanleys, seeing the way the battle was going, threw their forces behind Henry. They had waited to see who was going to win and made sure that at the crucial moment they were on that side. Henry was fortunate: not only had he been able to have the fate of the crown of England decided on a battlefield, where he stood his only chance, but he had killed Richard and therefore removed a source of future unrest.

Henry made sure that this advantage was driven home. He was quick to make his claim to the throne legitimate as he did not want it to be dependent upon his marriage to Elizabeth of York, nor on defeating Richard. Therefore he dated his reign from the day before Bosworth so that Richard and his supporters could be declared traitors and their estates could become the property of the crown through acts of attainder. He also ensured that his coronation was before parliament met, so that it could not be claimed that parliament had made him king. The marriage to Elizabeth did not take place until after his coronation, again ensuring that it could not be said that he owed the throne to his wife.

Henry's immediate concern was to keep the throne. Having seized the throne by force it was to be expected that he would have to face a number of challenges. Many Yorkists had been killed during the Wars of the Roses, but there were still a number alive with a good claim to the throne, certainly as good as, or better than, Henry Tudor's. Others had benefitted under the Yorkists and were also likely to plot and rise against the new king to try to regain their former positions and influence. Therefore, although Henry had achieved his first goal, there was a long way to go before he was secure.

2 The problem of the nobility

> **KEY ISSUE** How successful was Henry in controlling the nobility?

Some historians have suggested that, in order to secure the throne, Henry saw the nobility as a danger and that he set out to be ruthless towards them.[1] However, more recent work has shown that to survive he would need their support as they would be vital in controlling England effectively. Although many were disillusioned by the rule of Richard III, this did not mean that they would give their unequivocal support to Henry. He would have to prove that he could provide stability, security and justice if they were to back him. Their support would be crucial as Henry had little knowledge of England and would need their advice to be able to govern. He would need them to fill key offices in government and to run the shires and ensure that the royal writ was obeyed in the localities. The nobility were the only ones with sufficient political clout to be able to do this, and therefore the support of the gentry would not be enough. Henry was also aware that many of the nobles had supported Richard because they had done well under his rule and could provide the leadership needed to overthrow him if they felt excluded. Their support for a rebellion could, as Henry had himself discovered at Bosworth, be sufficient to turn the tide against the king and produce a successful rebellion. Moreover, Henry would have been well aware that some of the nobility had just as good a claim to the throne as he did. If he could seize it, perhaps they might try.

Henry used a variety of methods to win their support. He was willing to give all the nobility a chance to prove their loyalty, even those who had supported Richard at Bosworth. This was done by both bribes and threats. The Duke of Northumberland was released from gaol very quickly and given the chance to prove his loyalty by taking up his old position governing the north. However, Viscount Beauchmont had to pay financial sureties for his good behaviour. Although Henry was suspicious of Richard's supporters he was still willing to offer them a place on his Council. What mattered to Henry was loyalty, and if they were willing to be loyal he was willing to forget the past. However, many nobles were bound over to keep the peace under the threat of land loss if they did not. This was a particularly clever measure as the nobility saw their land holdings as their prized possession. Other leading nobles were forced to enter into bonds, recognizances or obligations which ordered them to remain loyal or to perform specific duties on pain of forfeiture. Henry went a long way towards disabling his nobility. He took a particularly strong line over the question of retainers. He severely limited the numbers who could keep an armed retinue until he was sure of their loyalty and allowed the numbers to grow only when he felt secure.

Despite these measures Henry faced a rebellion within one year of seizing the throne. However, it can be argued that this was almost inevitable and that Henry's measures were a success because the rising was never a serious threat to his position. The source of the trouble was some of Richard's old supporters, Lord Lovell and the Stafford brothers. The three had all been claiming sanctuary, but when Henry travelled north to visit his northern capital of York, they broke out. They planned to detain Henry, whilst also raising a rebellion in the west. However, Henry heard of the rising and sent an armed force to offer them a choice of pardon, or death, if they fought and lost. This was sufficient to disperse the rebels, but Lovell was able to flee to Flanders, whilst the Staffords sought sanctuary again. But this time they were arrested; one was executed, whilst the other received a pardon and remained loyal.

The execution was designed to be a clear warning to others who might contemplate rebellion. Henry was willing to show clemency but he was also prepared, where necessary, to be severe. The king continued his tour north, where his presence did much to win loyalty in an area with strong Yorkist traditions. However, although this rebellion had collapsed almost before it had begun, it would have worried Henry. He would have been unsure of how much Yorkist support the rebels might collect. It is much easier for historians than it would have been for Henry to conclude that if there were to be a successful rebellion it would need to have a Yorkist prince as its leader. But there were none available and so those who were opposed to Henry had to turn to candidates who could impersonate the Yorkist princes.

3 Lambert Simnel

> **KEY ISSUE** How serious a threat was Lambert Simnel to royal authority and the Tudor monarchy?

Henry faced many challenges to his authority, but perhaps the best known came from two pretenders to the throne, Lambert Simnel and Perkin Warbeck. Both rebellions show that Henry's hold on the crown was not secure in the early years. The challenge from Simnel came within one year of his seizure of the crown, whereas Warbeck's challenge was to last from 1491 to 1499, suggesting that perhaps Henry lacked the authority to deal firmly with the challenge. Although it could be argued that because the challenges had to come from pretenders Henry was not in a weak position, this seems to be a misinterpretation, for instead the credence and international support that was given to both suggest that Henry's position was vulnerable.

The Battle of Bosworth had seen the defeat of the Yorkist king, Richard III. It was therefore inevitable that the Yorkists and their supporters would mount a challenge to try to regain the throne. The problem was that there was no obvious candidate. It was for this reason that they turned to a pretender: Lambert Simnel. It had initially been the plan to pass him off as one of the murdered sons of Edward IV. However, rumours of the death of the Earl of Warwick led to a change of plan. Simnel would impersonate him. The whole of the Simnel story shows close links with the Yorkist cause. The rebellion had its roots in the Yorkist stronghold of Oxford and then Simnel was taken to Ireland, another Yorkist stronghold, where he was proclaimed Edward VI. This was a clever tactical move as the Irish nobility had always favoured the Yorkists and Henry had failed to confirm the Earl of Kildare as Lord Deputy of Ireland, alienating crucial elements in Irish society.

The problem soon became more serious because Edward IV's sister, Margaret of Burgundy, sent a force of 2,000 mercenaries from Germany to help Simnel. What should have been a minor irritant had started to take on a European dimension. Evidence also suggests that Henry was not aware of the rising until early 1487, despite the fact that it had begun in 1486, a further indication of his vulnerable position. Even then his difficulties did not go away. Henry was worried about the scale of support Simnel might receive if he landed in England and therefore he offered the rebels a pardon. At the same time, Henry paraded the real Warwick in London to show that Simnel was an impostor. Yet this did not stop the danger. In fact it grew more serious as the Earl of Lincoln fled to join the rebels.

The rising became a real challenge when, on 4 June 1487, Simnel and his army landed in Lancashire and began to march south. It was at this stage that Henry received his first piece of good news: Simnel did not get the support he expected. There are a number of possible reasons for this; firstly the country may have had enough of the chaos and disorder of the Wars of the Roses and did not want a further period of warfare. But there is also the view that they may simply have disliked the large Irish contingent, with their reputation for brutality, and decided to wait and see the outcome before deciding how to react. It is less likely that their acquiescence showed support for Henry, as later events would reveal.

As the two sides came face to face at Stoke, near Newark, Henry must have realised that the fate of his crown depended upon the vagaries of battle, in much the same way as it had at Bosworth some two years earlier. There are many similarities between the two events. Although Henry's force outnumbered the rebels by over 4,000, two wings of his army held back until they were certain that Henry would win. Even this had not been obvious at the outset as the initial rebel attack had seriously challenged the king's frontline. It was only after three hours that Henry was certain of victory. But even in victory Henry did not achieve all his aims. He had ordered his army to take the Earl of Lincoln alive, but this was not obeyed. This may have been because some on the king's side were concerned that, if he was captured, he would implicate them, whereas once dead this could not be revealed, suggesting that some of Henry's supporters were hedging their bets with a foot in both camps.

Although Henry was eventually successful it does not mean that the rising was doomed to failure. An impostor had been able to attract powerful backers and attract support in Ireland and England, showing how insecure the monarchy was. For a time Simnel was a menace. The fate of the Tudor dynasty had been decided by a battle, but the result could just as easily have been reversed. Henry was well aware of his weak position and soon took action to strengthen it. Firstly, he quickly married Elizabeth of York to try to secure goodwill. Then parliament deprived those nobles who had fought at Stoke of their lands and attainted them. However, closer examination suggests that the position was not quite as desperate. The rebels had failed to get the large numbers they expected in England, raising an overall force of only 8,000. In fact they were able to invade only because of Irish support. Moreover, the important fact was that Henry had won. He would never again face an army of his own people.

4 Perkin Warbeck

> **KEY ISSUES** Why did the challenge from Warbeck last so long?
> How serious was the challenge?

The origins of this rising are unclear, but is likely that, as in the case of Simnel, Margaret of Burgundy was behind the plot. In the same way that Simnel had made his way to Ireland, a centre for Yorkist plots, so did Warbeck. The plot was also a potential danger to Henry because of the international situation in which he was embroiled. Relations with both France and Scotland were poor and they could use the challenge of Warbeck to undermine the king. It was this that enabled the rebellion to drag on for so long, as foreign powers used Warbeck's nuisance value to exert diplomatic pressure on Henry.

At first it appeared that Henry's position was more secure than in 1486–7. Warbeck's arrival in Ireland was greeted with little enthusiasm, suggesting that Henry had gone some way to winning over their support since 1487. However, his appearance did impress some of the townspeople of Cork, who assumed that he was Earl of Warwick. Warbeck denied this and instead claimed that he was Richard Duke of York, who had supposedly been murdered in the Tower. This presented Henry with a problem. He could not parade the real Richard and disprove the claim as Richard was already dead. This was one reason why support for Warbeck lingered on.

Warbeck's failure to win large-scale support in Ireland encouraged him to try elsewhere. The usual problem areas were only too willing to exploit the opportunity and the problem soon became entangled with foreign relations. Warbeck's first destination was France, where he was welcomed at the royal court, and was soon joined by about 100 dissident Yorkists. However, this problem was soon resolved as the Treaty of Etaples of 1492 between England and France forced him to flee. Warbeck next tried his luck in Flanders, where he could count on the support of Margaret. It was obvious that Henry viewed the situation with alarm as his response was to break off trade, despite the damage that this caused to England's cloth trade. However, the position for Henry became even more desperate when Warbeck secured the backing of the Holy Roman Emperor, who recognised him as Richard IV. But fortunately for Henry the Emperor lacked the financial resources to act and France was soon diverted towards Italy. This meant that Henry could tackle the Warbeck problem without the threat of foreign invasion. He used the more favourable international situation to make a pre-emptive strike at those involved in England. Parliament was persuaded to pass a series of attainders, but it must have been worrying that one of those implicated was Stanley. He had helped Henry win the throne at Bosworth and was a close and influential friend. Clearly the king was still insecure. If Stanley could turn against the king, who else might?

However, the work of Henry's spies ensured that the possibility of the rising spreading was prevented. This meant that when Warbeck tried to land at Deal in July 1495 it was a fiasco. The local militia attacked with such force that the invaders were routed without help from royal troops. The rising had to be abandoned and Warbeck sailed to Ireland. Here he tried to take Waterford, but failed and moved on to Scotland, where he received an enthusiastic reception from the king and was married to the king's cousin. It has been suggested that this showed that the Scottish king believed Warbeck's claim. However, it is more likely that it simply illustrates the problems facing Henry: foreign rulers were willing to take advantage of any opportunity to weaken his position. The Scottish king, James, provided Warbeck with military aid so that by September he was able to cross the border with 1,500 troops, but after a few days of pillage he was forced to return to Scotland. Henry must have gained some comfort from the fact that no Englishmen had joined Warbeck. This was increased when Scotland signed a truce with England and Warbeck had to change bases again. Why had the Scots abandoned Warbeck? They had obviously decided that they would gain more from the proposed marriage between James and Henry's daughter. This decision may have been prompted by the fact that it was now obvious that Henry Tudor was not going to be stopped, and so there was little to be gained from continuing to support the pretender. Although this interpretation may be based on the benefit of hindsight, Henry must have realised that his position was becoming stronger.

Warbeck returned to Ireland but discovered that it too was loyal to Henry. Finally he set sail for England, hoping to exploit the disquiet in the South West (see pages 18–20). This final episode is noteworthy only for its pathetic ending. He was driven from both Exeter and Taunton and few locals joined the rising. Warbeck abandoned his followers and sought sanctuary at Beaulieu Abbey. However, in August 1497 he was persuaded to give himself up and confess. As a foreigner it would have been difficult to convict him of treason, so Henry allowed him to remain at court. But in 1498 he ran away; this time Henry was less lenient and had him put in the Tower. What happened next is still unclear. Whether he plotted with the Earl of Warwick or whether he was tricked by Henry is uncertain, but in 1499 he was accused of trying to escape and put on trial, found guilty and executed. This brought to an end the longest, but perhaps one of the weakest, challenges to the Tudor dynasty. However, Henry had to act to remove him because of pressure from the Spaniards, who wanted the Tudor dynasty to be secure before they allowed Catherine of Aragon to marry Prince Arthur.

The plot had never won much support in England and had been a danger only because of the use made of it by foreign powers. Without their help, it would not have dragged on for so long. It is likely that Warbeck's rising was part of a detailed plan by the Yorkists to regain the throne, rather than a spontaneous event. Although it is unlikely that he ever convinced anyone that he was Richard, the Yorkists saw in it their best chance of removing Henry and were willing to back anyone to gain revenge. Even though it failed it did cause Henry considerable embarrassment, and it was for that reason that he finally executed him. The revolt had easily been contained and Warbeck, unlike Simnel, had been unable to force the king into a pitched battle.

5 The Yorkshire and Cornish Rebellions

> **KEY ISSUES** What were the causes of these rebellions? Did they represent a challenge to royal authority?

Henry faced two major internal rebellions that threatened his authority.They were both caused by his need for money and by the heavy taxation demands that he made. They were both important because they had an impact on the way that he responded to other threats.

The first challenge was in Yorkshire in 1489. Henry had planned to help Brittany in this Duchy's struggle against France. Parliament had granted him money for this, but the tax was raised in a new way and this caused resentment, particularly in the north. The population there had suffered a series of bad harvests and were not used to heavy taxation. Added to this, the French threat was of little concern to them and they did not expect to have to pay for what was, in their minds, a southern issue. They had usually been exempt from taxation because of the cost of defending the frontier from the Scottish danger. However, Henry refused to negotiate, and when the Earl of Northumberland tried to collect the tax he was murdered. Historians have usually attributed this to his support for the unpopular tax, particularly as the man accused of the murder, Sir John Egremont, led the subsequent rebellion. However, it is also possible that Egremont saw the unpopularity of the tax as an opportunity to further the Yorkist cause as he was an illegitimate member of the Percy family and a Yorkist sympathiser. The murder of royal officials engaged in implementing unpopular policies was not unusual and was often the only way for the community to show its displeasure. Soon a rebel force was assembled, but it was defeated by a royal army outside York and Egremont was forced to flee.

The rebellion had been easily defeated and Henry would not face any more trouble from the region. One of the reasons for the tranquility of the north, however, was that the new Earl of Northumberland was a minor. However, Henry failed to raise any of the tax. This was a clear indication that ruling England required compromise and negotiation, something for which the years in exile had not prepared the king. It also showed that order in many areas was fragile and could soon erupt into a direct challenge to royal authority. The king was aware of this as he appointed the Earl of Surrey as his lieutenant in the area, a man with no interests in the north but completely loyal to the Tudors as the restoration of his own lands depended upon his succeeding here.

The other, more serious challenge was also brought about because of Henry's financial needs. The Cornish revolt of 1497 had many similarities with the Yorkshire rebellion. Once again parliament had granted the king money, this time to fight Warbeck. Now it was the

Cornish who refused to pay on the grounds that the tax had nothing to do with them as Warbeck's challenge was coming from Scotland. Once again this was a clear sign of the local thinking of English society in this period, and, as in the north, a sign that not all areas of England had been absorbed into the nation. However, the rising was more serious than the threat from Yorkshire because it overlapped with Warbeck's challenge.

The rebels left Bodmin in May 1497 and set off, in an orderly fashion, to present their grievances to the king. They marched through Cornwall, where they gained support from members of the clergy and well established gentry. However, they failed to gain support in Devon, a sign of the antagonism between the two counties and a further indication of the localised thinking that characterised the period. Only when they entered Somerset did they gain further support. The numbers who were prepared to leave their locality shows that there was widespread support for the rebellion, and the cross-section of society involved is a clear indication that the rebels' grievances cut across class barriers. However, they were able to gain the backing of only one member of the nobility, Lord Audley. He was not typical of his class as he was in a state of penury and this may have been a last desperate gamble to try to repair the family fortunes.

By the time the rebels reached Guildford their numbers had swelled to 15,000. They must have presented a serious threat to Henry, who was also faced with the challenge from Warbeck. It must also have been a matter of concern to the king that the rebels had been able to march so far without being challenged. However, as they came closer to London their numbers began to decrease as many began to desert, either fearful of being so far from home or worried by the outcome of facing a substantial royal force. The remaining men made their way to Blackheath, the traditional meeting place of aggrieved peasants. In traditional fashion the rebels made it clear that their complaints were against 'evil counsellors', rather than the king – a theme that would be echoed throughout the sixteenth century. This time those counsellors were Morton and Bray, who were blamed for the excessive financial demands. However, Henry took no chances and by June, when the rebels were at Blackheath, he had assembled a force of 25,000 men. It was therefore hardly surprising that the rebellion was crushed. The king was able to get his forces behind the rebels and allow his archers and cavalry to wreak havoc. Contemporary estimates suggest that over 1,000 rebels were killed and the rest fled in panic.

Henry did not view the rebellion as a serious threat and only two local leaders and the Earl of Audley were executed. The king was correct in his assessment: the rebels had only been able to get so far because Henry had been more concerned with the challenge from Warbeck because of his links with the Yorkist challenge, whilst the Cornish rebels had no such links. But it had shown that areas of the kingdom were still not prepared to finance a campaign to defend the Tudor monarchy. However, some historians have suggested that the causes of the rebellion were more complex, making it a greater threat. They have suggested that it was also a protest against local government officials in the region who were corrupt and were seen to be failing in their administrative duties, therefore creating resentment against the government. The severity of the king's response at Blackheath shows that not only was he determined to crush the rising once and for all, but that he viewed it as a challenge to his authority. This time there was no second chance, as Simnel had been given: the leaders were captured and executed and those involved were fined heavily.

Even those who did not join the rebel cause may have kept out only because they were disillusioned with unrest, not because they supported the king. Therefore it can be concluded that, even after 15 years on the throne, Hency could command only limited loyalty.

6 Later challenges

KEY ISSUE When did Henry feel secure?

Fortunately for Henry, many of the potential claimants to the throne had been killed either during the Wars of the Roses or early in his reign. The Earl of Warwick had been executed a week after Warbeck, and so the nearest Yorkist claimant was now the Earl of Suffolk. It might therefore be reasonable to assume that Henry's position was secure, but this was not the case. Although the Earl of Suffolk appeared to be loyal there were underlying tensions and distrust. His brother, the Earl of Lincoln, had been killed at the Battle of Stoke and the Earl was dissatisfied because Henry would not create him Duke of Suffolk, like his father. As a result he suddenly fled to France in 1499, but Henry persuaded him to return. However, in 1501 he fled again, this time to the court of the Emperor, Maximilian. The Emperor's court soon became a focus for other Yorkists who joined him, whilst Maximilian was only too willing to encourage another Yorkist plot.

At the same time Henry's position at home was weakened. In 1500 his third son died and then, in 1502, Arthur, the heir to the throne, also died. This meant that the Tudor succession depended upon his ten-year-old son, Henry. Matters were made worse in 1503 when Henry VII's wife died. In response to these events Henry began to look for a new wife and to take further drastic action against potential enemies. Members of the Suffolk family who were still in England were imprisoned, whilst the Parliament of 1504 passed 51 attainders, more than any other parliament of his reign. The list included Sir James Tyrell, who had been Constable of the Tower. Before his death he confessed to the murder of Edward IV's sons, the 'Princes in the Tower', thus making it difficult for future impostors.

Despite this Henry could still not feel secure about the succession. One of his officials told him of a conversation at Calais where there was a discussion of what would happen when the king died:

> Some of them spoke of my lord of Buckingham, saying that he was a noble man and would be a royal ruler. Others who were that spoke in a similar manner about your traitor, Edmund de la Pole, but none of them spoke of my lord prince Henry.

If this was indeed the view of the political nation it showed just how insecure the Tudor dynasty might be.

However, in 1506 Henry's luck finally appeared to change. Storms forced Philip of Burgundy to land in England and Henry was able to persuade him to hand over the Earl of Suffolk. Henry had to agree to spare his life, but at least the Earl was safely in the Tower. Henry Tudor could at last feel secure, but the future of the dynasty depended upon the health of one son.

7 Conclusion

> **KEY ISSUE** How secure was Henry VII?

Although it was not until the latter years of his reign that Henry VII could feel secure, he was never seriously challenged. However, it is the benefit of hindsight that allows historians to see that the Battle of Bosworth was the end of the Wars of the Roses and not the start of another series of struggles for the throne of England. The Yorkists were not reconciled to his rule and it is no surprise that the most serious revolts that he faced were those with dynastic links. The greatest challenge was that of Simnel, because it came so soon after Bosworth and forced Henry to fight another battle before he could be certain of support. However, it is important not to exaggerate the dynastic threat facing Henry. He was fortunate in that there was an absence of males of royal blood, unlike the situation under Edward IV, with the result that there was no obvious focus for political discontent.[2] Simnel and Warbeck tried to dress their goals in dynastic terms, but it could be argued that the most serious rebellion was the Cornish Rising, which was not dynastic in origin. Its success in moving so far across the country and away from its home region shows that Henry's tax demands were resented and suggests that his handling of the local gentry was insensitive, as these men should have stopped the rising at an earlier stage.

Throughout his reign Henry was concerned about the security of his throne. This was largely the result of him having seized the throne by force and a realisation that his claim to the throne was so weak. If he could take the crown by force so could others, particularly if they were able to secure the support of foreign powers.

References

1 Christine Carpenter, *The Wars of the Roses*, (CUP, 1997), p. 242.
2 John Guy, *Tudor England* (OUP, 1988), p. 58.

Summary Diagram
How Secure was Henry VII? Inheritance and Taxation

DATE	STRENGTH?	WEAKNESS?	
		INHERITANCE	TAXATION
1485	BATTLE OF BOSWORTH		
1486	MARRIAGE TO ELIZABETH OF YORK	REBELLION OF LOVELL AND STAFFORD	
1486–7		LAMBERT SIMNEL (help from Ireland, Burgundy & Lovell)	
1489		Egremont's role? ◄———►	YORKSHIRE
1491–9		PERKIN WARBECK (help from Ireland, Burgundy, France, Scotland & Stanleys)	
1497			CORNISH RISING
1499–1506			
1501	MARRIAGE OF PRINCE ARTHUR	SUFFOLK'S REBELLION	
1502		DEATH OF PRINCE ARTHUR	
1503		DEATH OF ELIZABETH OF YORK	

Answering structured questions on Chapter 2

One of the new features of the AS specification has been the introduction of the structured question, rather than candidates simply
writing an essay on a particular topic. These new types of question
demand a specific approach if you are to achieve good marks.
Study the following questions:
Explain two reasons why Henry VII faced challenges to his throne in the
early years of his reign. (*30 marks*)
How serious a threat to royal authority were the rebellions under Henry
VII? (*60 marks*)

The first thing to note is that each question carries a different number of marks. It is important not to write too much for part a) and not leave sufficient time for part b). Examiners would expect you to write between one and one and a half sides for part a) and about three sides for part b).

When tackling part a) it is important to pay attention to the instructions contained in the question. You are asked to explain two reasons: do not therefore waste time on more, as you will not gain credit for any extra reasons that you give. Also ensure that you explain reasons why Henry faced challenges, rather than describe what the challenges were. If you just describe what happened you will reach only the lower bands in the mark schemes. In order to reach the higher levels it may be helpful to start your writing as follows: 'There were challenges because ...' or 'Henry VII faced challenges because ...'. In this question your two points may be the weakness of his claim to the throne and the power of the nobility. You would want to explain that his claim was based on military victory and therefore others with a claim might also try to gain the throne. You would also need to explain how tenuous his claim to throne was, and this requires a knowledge of the Tudor family tree. When considering the power of the nobility you might consider the legacy of the Wars of the Roses and the development of private armies.

As far as question b) is concerned, the important element is 'How serious'. The question requires you to evaluate the challenges that Henry faced. You must also ensure that you draw your examples from the whole of his reign and not just the start. Better answers will draw attention to the change in royal authority during the course of the reign, showing that during the latter years he was more secure. It would also be important to examine the different challenges that Henry faced: some rebellions aimed at his overthrow, whilst others were protests against particular policies and were therefore less of a threat. You might also want to consider the importance of foreign help and whether that made certain challenges a greater threat. There is plenty of material available and it will be important to organise your material in a coherent fashion. Do not try to write everything you know: examiners would much rather have a well argued, analytical answer, than an attempt to cover everything.

3 Henry VIII: The Powerful Monarch?

POINTS TO CONSIDER

This chapter gives a brief summary of the early years of Henry VIII's reign before concentrating on what many have considered the greatest threat to any Tudor monarch, the Pilgrimage of Grace. It examines the possible causes of the rebellion before concluding with a consideration of its importance. You will need to evaluate the causes and consider how serious a challenge the rebellion presented.

KEY DATES

1509 The Accession of Henry VIII.
Henry VIII's marriage to Catherine of Aragon.
1516 Birth of Princess Mary.
1523 Parliament grants only half Wolsey's subsidy for the war against France.
1525 Francis I, King of France, is captured by Charles V. Henry wants to attack France, but attempts to raise money result in resistance.
1527 Henry announces his intention to divorce Catherine.
1529 Opening of the Reformation Parliament.
1532 Thomas Cranmer appointed Archbishop of Canterbury.
1533 Henry marries Anne Boleyn and marriage to Catherine is declared void.
1534 Thomas Cromwell appointed Vice-Regent in charge of church affairs.
1536 Dissolution of the smaller monasteries. 10 Articles and Injunctions suggest a more Protestant direction.
Lincolnshire Rising and Pilgrimage of Grace.
1537 Risings in the North West.
1538 Thirteen Articles and new set of Royal Injunctions suggests a catholic revival.
1539 Act of Six Articles, further catholic moves.
1540 Fall of Thomas Cromwell.
1543 The King's Book, reinforces catholic belief.

1 Introduction

Traditional textbooks have portrayed Henry as a strong and ruthless monarch who expected to be obeyed and sought vengeance on any who questioned his authority. However, a closer examination of his reign shows that he faced similar problems to other Tudor monarchs and that ruling England, even in the sixteenth century, required skill and compromise. Nonetheless, his early years were relatively peaceful.

This was due to a number of reasons. Firstly, few lamented the passing of Henry VII, for in his latter years had been inaccessible and his reign had been characterised by heavy taxation. Henry VIII made immediate moves to distance himself from his father and win popularity. He arrested and later executed the two men most closely associated with the heavy financial burdens of his father's reign. Secondly, Henry VIII, in contrast to his father, was not a mean old man: instead he was a true Renaisance prince who was willing to spend and make merry, thus winning himself popularity with many in the political nation. Lastly, the Tudor monarchy was more secure and if Henry VII had achieved anything it was to rid the country of potential challengers to the throne. However, although Henry VIII might expect unquestioned obedience, in practice he did not always receive it. On two occasions, as the early goodwill was exhausted and major changes were introduced, he faced serious challenges to his power, the first in 1525, over taxation, and the second in 1536, with the more complex Pilgrimage of Grace.

2 The Early Years

> **KEY ISSUE** What can we learn about the power of Tudor monarchs from the failure to raise the Amicable Grant?

a) Background

As Henry VII's reign had shown, heavy taxation had sometimes prompted rebellion, or at least passive resistance, and the reign of his son was no different. Just like his father, Henry VIII waged war; as with his father, this meant an increase in the tax burden; and, as with his father again, this resulted in protest. It was the commonly held view that monarchs should 'live of their own': that is government should, and could, be paid for from the king's traditional income without asking parliament. The only time parliament should have to raise taxes was in a time of emergency, usually war. Early in his reign Henry had provoked passive resistance in the north of England by taxing the people in order to fight the Scots. The situation in 1525 was somewhat different. In 1523 the king's chief minister, Wolsey, had asked parliament for the enormous sum of £800,000. This was far in excess of anything levied before and beyond the willingness, or capability, of the nation. In the end £150,000 had been collected by the spring of 1525.

b) The Amicable Grant

In 1525 Henry wanted to launch an attack against France. The king of France, Francis I, had been captured by Charles V whilst fighting in Italy. Henry saw that, with the French king in captivity, it was the ideal time for him to stake his claim to the French throne and prove himself to be the heir to Henry V. In order to fulfil his ambition he needed to raise a large sum of money. However, his demands must be seen in the context of the demands made in 1523 and only recently collected. Many people felt that they had already paid sufficient in recent years; according to Scarisbrick, the collectors 'came upon lambs already close shorn'.[1] The people also questioned the benefit of a further French campaign as nothing of substance had been achieved in previous attempts to take the throne.

Henry, on the other hand, needed to act quickly and this only added to his difficulties. Commissions to raise the money were sent out only at the end of March, yet the tax was to be collected by early June. Tudor government did not work that fast and this added to the unpopularity of the request. The collection made little progress; Warwickshire was soon exempted from payment and this was followed by reports of problems in East Anglia, Berkshire, Wiltshire and Kent. Wolsey tried to solve the problems by stating that he would accept what communities could afford, rather than the sum that had been fixed. However, instead of resolving the problem it hardened attitudes. People realised that the government had, to some extent, backed down: therefore if they continued to resist they might be able to gain even greater concessions.

Faced by a serious rising in the area around the borders of Suffolk and Essex, the government did indeed renounce its plans. Henry announced that the grant had been abandoned and the ringleaders of the resistance were pardoned. In a further sign of defeat Wolsey had to lead a ceremony of reconciliation, begging the king to pardon his fellow Suffolk men for the disturbances.

The rebellion had ended in a government climb-down and the abandonment of the invasion of France. The protest had shown that it was possible to force the government to abandon an unpopular policy. Yet questions remain. Why had the government changed its policy? What does this tell us about the power of Tudor government? The successful protest had been possible because of large-scale opposition to the grant and because support for the protest involved a cross section of society, not just the commons. This showed that when the crown was robbed of its traditional supporters, namely the wealthy, it was vulnerable because this group were those who traditionally defended the monarchy against disorder. It was a lesson that was not lost on the leaders of the Pilgrimage of Grace (pages 27–39). Moreover, the government was faced with opposition spread over several counties, and rumours of further resistance encouraged those who were already in revolt to harden their attitude. Meanwhile those who were contemplating rising were encouraged by the scale of resistance. In other words, once the rising was under way it appeared to fuel itself. Two other factors added to the rebels' success. Firstly, London, which was usually loyal, was adamant that it would not pay.

Faced with opposition at the centre of the kingdom, the government had to take the matter seriously. Secondly, those councillors who had been charged with the collection of the Grant were quick to report opposition, rather than try to deal with it. As a consequence the government received a large amount of news of resistance, and this also encouraged them to reconsider the grant.

3 The Pilgrimage of Grace

> **KEY ISSUE** What can we learn about the causes of the risings from the actions of the rebels?

a) Introduction

In the late autumn and early winter of 1536–7 Henry VIII faced the greatest challenge to his power. These events have become known as the Pilgrimage of Grace. However, to be technically correct the term should be applied only to the risings in the north of England between October and December 1536, but it has also been used to cover two other disturbances: the Lincolnshire Rising of October 1536 and the Cumberland rising of 1537. The Pilgrimage is probably the best documented of all the Tudor risings. Many of those involved in the rising wrote detailed accounts, but until recently the major work on the Pilgrimage was by Ruth and Madeleine Dodds, written in 1915, which provided a full and detailed account of the events. But recent research by Michael Bush has challenged many of the Dodds', and other historians', interpretations and resulted in a reassessment of the significance of the rising.[2] Although there is controversy surrounding both the causes of the disturbances and their significance, historians agree about what took place in the autumn of 1536.

b) The Lincolnshire Rising

In many ways the Lincolnshire rising was a prelude to the Pilgrimage of Grace, providing the pilgrims with many of their grievances. The Lincolnshire rising started in early October 1536 and although it was over in a fortnight it inspired and gave the pilgrims an example of how to raise a large-scale rebellion. Although the rebels dispersed easily they presented the government with a serious challenge for two reasons. Firstly, it was not just caused by the commons, but was led, and even instigated, by the gentry and well-to-do; secondly, the rebels were able to raise a significant force of perhaps 40,000 men very quickly. As a consequence the government was forced to bring in outside troops to put down the rising.

Lincolnshire was a hot-bed of rumours in the autumn of 1536 as three government commissions were at work: the first overseeing the closure of the smaller monasteries, the second assessing and collecting the 1534 subsidy and the third examining the state of the clergy. The activities of these commissioners created further rumours of new taxes, the seizure of goods and even the closure of some churches. It was therefore hardly surprising that when a commissioner arrived at the town of Louth, where the people were very proud of their new church spire, he was seized by men guarding the church and its treasure. This was the signal for a full-scale rising to begin. Paid from church funds, a local force was assembled and its numbers soon swelled as beacons, bells and word of mouth spread the news of the rising. Within days a force of some 40,000 well armed and disciplined men had been assembled. Their first action was to march to Lincoln where most of the city welcomed them. Here they drew up a set of articles and sent them to London. However, when the king's reply reached Lincoln, threatening severe punishments if they did not disperse, the leadership was forced to make a choice. They now knew that further resistance was treason, that a large royal army was on the way and that the chances of victory for them were remote. Therefore they seized the opportunity of the first offer that was made: namely that the king would consider their demands if they went home peacefully. As a result, by the time the royal force arrived there was no rebellion to overcome as the rebels had returned home. However, Henry wanted the rebels crushed and their leaders executed for their failure to remain loyal. But events further north meant that he would have to wait for his wish to be put into practice.

c) Whose rebellion was the Lincolnshire rising?

We have already suggested that the rising was led, even if not instigated, by the gentry. Yet these were the very men whom the government would normally have expected to put down a rebellion. However, not all gentry took part willingly; some were seized and threatened with the loss of goods, or even their life, if they did not take part. It would have been very difficult to have resisted such demands, a fact which suggests that many of the gentry were coerced into taking part. On the other hand, some of the gentry certainly tried to control the rising as the priest Nicholas Leche testified in his examination:

> 1 He thinks all the exterior acts of the gentlemen along with the commons were done willingly, for he saw them as willing to set forward their views in the same way as the commons were. And further, during the whole time of the insurrection, not one of the gentlemen persuaded
> 5 the people to stop or showed them it was high treason ... The gentlemen were first armed of all the people, and commanded the commons to prepare themselves, and he believes the commons expected to have redress of grievances by way of request to the king.

Some of those involved argued that the rebels did nothing without

The spire of Louth Church on which the inhabitants spent £305, which was a great deal of money then.

the permission of the gentry, but this can be seen as a sign of respect for their superior social position. Many of the gentry wrote to the king arguing that their plan was to gain control of the rising, but this may have been to try to excuse their behaviour. There is also the possibility that the gentry became involved in order to prevent the commons from becoming too destructive and excessive in their demands: after all, the gentry had the most to lose and were fearful of the destruction of their property and goods should the rebels get out of hand. This interpretation does appear to be plausible as they soon came to an agreement with the king when an opportunity presented itself.

There is little doubt that the clergy and monks played a significant role in the rising. This was hardly surprising as the church had suffered most from the changes under Cromwell and had every reason to believe that further change was possible. They supported their concerns with money, providing the Louth rebels with funds. There is also evidence that the parish clergy helped to mobilise the movement, and monks from some of the local monasteries joined, armed and horsed.

Yet the commons also had a great deal to fear: their lives were changing rapidly and there is little doubt that they believed further change was likely. But it is difficult to ascertain their exact role. The social structure of society meant that they would automatically look to their superiors for leadership and involvement in order to give the movement a sense of legitimacy. They would also want the gentry to articulate their views and express them to those in authority. Even at a time of unrest they wanted and expected leadership from their superiors.

As with many Tudor rebellions it is almost impossible to be certain about the motives of the rebels. Perhaps our clearest understanding comes from its symbols. When the Horncastle rebels reached home they placed their banner in their church and an examination of it reveals the complexity of the rising. The banner depicted the five wounds of Christ, a chalice, a plough and a horn. Although historians continue to disagree about the symbolism it is possible to argue that the banner shows that all three estates were united against the king. The chalice was the sign of the clergy, the plough the commons and the hunting horn of the nobility. If this is true it shows the complex interrelationship between the different social groups and should make us very wary of any simple explanation of the causes of this rising, as of others.

d) The Pilgrimage of Grace

The Pilgrimage started on October 8th, whilst the Lincolnshire rising was still under way, and lasted until a pardon was issued on December 6th. Lincolnshire provided the pilgrims with both inspiration and an example, and the Pilgrimage was very similar in many ways to the events further south, as the rebels recruited from all social groups and were led by local gentry. The armies were paid for from donations, particularly from the church and all those involved took an oath. It is very important to have a clear understanding of what happened as the actions of the rebels reveal just as much about the causes as the lists of grievances that they issued. In order to get a clear grasp it may help to see the rising in three phases: the first in October when the people mobilised, the second in November when a truce was arranged, and the final phase in December that culminated in a general pardon. The rising began in South Yorkshire and was soon under the control of Robert Aske. He provided the rising with leadership of high quality. Aske was a member of a leading Yorkshire family, but was also a lawyer who had experience of London as well as the north. He brought intelligence, skill in debating and argument and excellent organisational skills to the rising, thus ensuring that the large force under his command remained well disciplined and appeared as an army, rather than an uncontrollable rabble. It was Aske who provided the rising with its name, 'the Pilgrimage of Grace', a superb piece of propaganda, ensuring that it would appeal to the widest possible number, and he ensured that copies of the oath taken by the Lincolnshire men were distributed and taken by all those involved in the rising.

By October 16th Aske with a force of some 10,000 men had entered York where he was welcomed by the citizens. Soon the mayor had handed over the town and Aske had sent him a copy of the rebels' demands, which were very similar to those of the Lincolnshire rising. However, we must remember that other areas also rose, so that at his height there were nine regional armies in the north covering Northumberland, Durham, North Yorkshire and Cumberland. This was a great military achievement and it meant that the Pilgrimage became a serious military threat with some 30,000 well-armed men who had taken the oath. The armies were led by nobles or gentry. Lord Latimer and Sir Christopher Danby took Barnard Castle and then proceeded to pillage the Bishop of Durham's castle at Bishop Auckland. Although there was less support for the rising west of the Pennines, where the Earl of Derby supported the king, musters took place at Kirkby Stephen and Penrith in Westmorland.

The government was not prepared for such a large scale rising, many of Henry's forces being still in Lincolnshire dealing with the aftermath of the troubles there. Meanwhile another royal force under the Earl of Shrewsbury had reached Nottingham and was waiting for orders. In the north the important royal castle of Pontefract was under the command of Lord Darcy. He sent south for help, arguing that the castle was in poor condition and that the loyalty of the 300 troops there was dubious. A week later, on October 21st, Pontefract surrendered without a single blow. However, Darcy's support for the rising and his production of badges for the pilgrims confirmed Henry's fears about his loyalty.

Meanwhile Aske's force of 30,000 made its way to Pontefract where, on October 27th, they met the Duke of Norfolk and his force of 8,000. Although some of the pilgrims wanted to fight, Aske dissuaded them and proceeded to negotiate with Norfolk, showing that his purpose was not a military-style campaign. The demands made by the pilgrims were quite vague and Norfolk was able to win over their confidence. It was agreed that the pilgrims would send two representatives to London to present their demands to the king.

The pilgrimage now entered its second phase. Whilst they awaited the king's reply there was an uneasy truce between the two forces. Henry responded by rejecting the demands of the rebels, arguing that they were too vague and asking for their clarification to be given to Norfolk. However, in an attempt to end the rising he promised a pardon to all, except the ringleaders, hoping that this would be sufficient to persuade the rebels to disperse as had happened in Lincolnshire. At the same time he instructed Norfolk to agree to their demands whilst he considered what to do. Meanwhile Bowes and Ellerker had returned from their meeting with the king and assured the Pilgrims of Henry's good faith. This encouraged them to clarify their demands and allowed the rising to enter its final phase.

This began with Henry instructing Norfolk to issue a general pardon to prolong the truce and with the pilgrims issuing their 24 articles. These were drawn up by Aske in consultation with Darcy, but were then approved by all the pilgrim captains so that they contained the views of the whole north. The articles were then taken to Norfolk. He promised that the issues would be discussed in a parliament that would be called in the north. The next day Aske announced the terms to the pilgrims, who were convinced that they had won a great victory. Norfolk had convinced them that the king was grateful to the rebels for opening his eyes to the problems. As a result the pardon was issued and the pilgrims began to disperse. Aske himself submitted. He now travelled to London at the king's request where he was received with honour and showered with gifts. Whilst with Henry he wrote down all that had happened so that the king was better informed. Aske had in fact fallen for a confidence trick and this was further shown when he returned north and spoke of the good faith of the monarch. It appeared as if the rising was over and the pilgrims had scored a success in forcing the king to agree to their demands. However, events in Cumberland were to change the situation.

4 The Causes of the Pilgrimage of Grace

KEY ISSUE Was the Pilgrimage of Grace only a religious rising?

a) Introduction

When writing their account of the Pilgrimage of Grace the Dodds believed that they had found the true cause of the rising. They argued that it was an attempt to reverse the religious changes that Henry had carried out. There is certainly much evidence to support this view, as many of the rebels acted as if they were primarily motivated by religious factors. However, over recent years historians have questioned this assumption and suggested that there were other, more significant factors at work. In a very important article Geoffrey Elton suggested that 'the religious purposes of the Pilgrimage had shallow roots, except amongst the few who dominated its ideology, eloquence and propaganda.'[3] If religion was not the cause, what was? The arguments have centered on two other possible causes: namely economic and political. In this section we will examine these three interpretations of the rising and consider which, if any, of the views appears to offer the best explanation for this most serious challenge to the rule of Henry.

b) Religion

At first glance religion does appear to be the prime cause of the rising. This interpretation is supported by both the name given to the rising and much of the symbolism associated with it. The banner that the rebels carried depicted the five wounds of Christ and indicated that the pilgrims fought for Christ's cause, and the oath that all the rebels took also contained the statement that they were undertaking the pilgrimage in the name of Christ. Even the chronology of events appears to support this view: the rising occurred immediately after the closure of some of the smaller monasteries, and whilst commissioners were still at work closing others. This view has been supported in recent years by historians such as John Guy[4] and Christopher Haigh[5] who showed that in Lancashire the first areas to rise and the last to be quietened were those around the dissolved houses. The rebels' grievances also appear to support this interpretation. The religious grievances are at the head of the list of their demands and they make up nine out of 24 of their demands issued at Pontefract.

There is perhaps little surprise in this as the church had undergone massive upheaval in recent years, and now both monks and some clergy feared for their very livelihoods. Many monks had been made homeless and unemployed. What other response was available to them? They probably feared that they would be unable to cope in the outside world from which they had been isolated for many years. Undoubtedly they lacked the financial means to survive as they were given minimal pensions and had few skills to offer in a fast changing society. They were able to get a great deal of support from local people as very often the monks themselves came from the local area and would therefore have been known to the inhabitants. At the same

Banner of 5 Wounds

time many locals did not like the religious changes that were taking place. Although they did not understand many of the changes, they affected their lives considerably. Traditional religion that had sustained their lives was changing. They loved and contributed to the maintenance of their parish church and they feared all of this was under threat. Religion affected all aspects of their lives. Their year was governed by the church and its festivals. In particular they would have disliked the abolition of Holy Days as they were holidays and times of festivity, an escape from their harsh routines. The new taxes on baptism, burial and marriage would also have been resented as the poorer elements in the community were unable to pay them and it was believed that this would prevent their salvation. They were probably also worried by rumours of further religious changes which would have an even greater impact on their lives: there were stories circulating that some churches would be closed and that jewel and plate would be confiscated. Both of these would be a disaster: closure of the local church would mean a long walk to the nearest place of worship, whilst the local community had probably bought most of the jewels and plate, and would resent its seizure by central government.

The locals would also have been concerned about the closure of monasteries as often they provided the local place of worship and the provision for the teaching of God's word. Their closure would have a direct effect on their ability to obtain salvation and to be spiritually nurtured. They would also miss the many other functions that monasteries fulfilled (see pages 36–7).

At a deeper level, and as clear sign that the grievance were drawn up by the higher echelons of society, there is evidence to suggest that the doctrinal changes and apparent moves away from catholicism were resented. The rebels' grievances contain complaints against some of the reformist bishops who had been appointed, such as Cranmer, whilst there are also attacks against some of the European reformers such as Bucer and Melanchthon and many other obscure names as well:

> The first complaint concerns our religion: to have the heresies of Luther, Wycliffe, Huss, Melanchthon, ... the works of Tyndale, of Barnes, of Marshall, of Rastall, St.German and such other Anibaptist heresies within this realm annulled and destroyed.
>
> *(The Pontefract Articles, 1536)*

It is very unlikely that the names of many of these reformers would have been heard of by the commons, and therefore they suggest that it was the gentry who drew up the list of demands.

Aske may have made religion the central feature and main cause of the rising. It enabled him to rally a large section of the population behind him. Many of the ordinary people disliked the religious changes and, by portraying the rising in this way, he was able to appeal to the maximum number of potential supporters; a rising under any other name would have limited its appeal. Therefore although religion played a significant role in the grievances and the symbols, we must be careful not to assume it was not the only cause.

c) Economic Causes

Economic hardship had provided the motivation for earlier rebellions, most noticeably the successful resistance to the Amicable Grant of 1525 (see pages 25–7). However, a poor economic situation in the north of the country was not new and, in these circumstances, it is possible to suggest that rebellion for economic reasons might have taken place in almost every year of the century. If we are to see economic causes as a major factor the historian must be able to demonstrate a link between a bad economic situation and the rising and also that 1536 was a particularly bad year compared with years when there were no rebellions.

It is certainly true that the north was suffering from poverty and hunger at this time. The harvest of 1535 had been disastrous and 1536 had seen little improvement. These problems were exacerbated by the demands of taxation. In particular we know that there were complaints against the 1534 subsidy that was being collected. This tax aroused controversy: it had traditionally only been levied at a time of war but was now being levied in peace time and was therefore not seen as justified. There were also rumours of new taxes on sheep and cattle. Bad weather meant that livestock numbers were already low and a further tax threatened to increase the hardship that farmers already faced.

Two other economic developments may have played a role in the rising of the commons. The first was entry fines, which were taxes payable to the landowner upon the death of a tenant and the succession of his heir. With prices rising, owners were taking advantage of the entry fine system and substantially increasing the amount payable. This was very unpopular at a time when other hardships were already putting a stress on the position of the tenantry. The second problem was that of enclosure. However, we have to be very clear that this affected only certain areas of the revolt. Enclosure had only recently been introduced in the north west and was causing a grievance in the communities of the West Riding and the Lake areas. In particular it was bringing about further hardships in the more densely populated areas, for instance around York, where the process was putting pressure on the limited availability of land. But in most of the other areas where the rebellion occurred there is little evidence of conflict and most enclosure was settled in an amicable manner.

The government had also recently introduced the Statute of Uses. This may have been a factor in gentry involvement as, prior to this piece of legislation, the gentry had distributed their land among trustees. Through this process they had been able to avoid paying duty when their heir succeeded as the land was not held freehold. The act had prevented this process and forced the gentry to pay their feudal dues. If this was a factor, and according to the articles the rebels drew up at York it was, it was relevant only in the case of the gentry. Uses would not have affected the commons: in fact it is more than likely that the commons would not have understood their meaning. Perhaps it is a further indicator of the gentry using the commons to help put across their own complaints.

In the section above on religion much of the discussion centered on the dissolution of the monasteries. However, we must be aware that this event also had serious economic consequences for the north.

Monasteries played a pivotal role in the local economy. This was particularly true during times of need when they provided help and charity for those who were suffering economic hardships. At the same time they often provided locals with employment on monastic estates. This economic role was made clear by Aske at his interview after the rising when he stated that:

1   The said people had their bodies well fed by the monasteries; and
     many of their tenants were fed there, and serving men were well looked
     after in time of need by the abbeys; and now not only these tenants and
     servants lack the chance to be looked after there, and receive either
5   meat, cloth and wages, and they do not know how they will get a living.
     Also travellers and carriers of corn between Yorkshire, Lancashire,
     Kendall, Westmoreland and the bishopric of Durham benefited from the
     monasteries, the abbeys looked after and cared for both the horses and
     men, for no-one in these parts was denied, so that the people were well
10   looked after by the said abbeys.

The Examination of Robert Aske, 1537.

He went on to talk about other roles that the abbeys played in the local economy; those near to the coast maintained sea walls and dykes, whilst others ensured that bridges and highways were built and kept in a useable condition. In areas of poverty the monasteries were the only institution who had the money to carry out such repairs, which were vital in stimulating the local economy. At the same time we must not forget the more traditional tasks undertaken by monasteries: providing shelter for travellers, education and the safe deposit for valuable documents.

In light of this it would seem unwise to ignore economic factors as a cause of the rising, and historians such as A.G. Dickens have even suggested that 'the roots of the movement were decidedly economic, its demands predominantly secular, its interests in Rome almost negligible and its leading repressors were not Protestant merchants, but the highest nobility in the land who shared its hostile view against heresy'.[6]

d) Political causes

It was the work of G.R. Elton that first suggested that the Pilgrimage was caused by political factors. He stated that 'the Pilgrimage originated in a decision by one of the court factions to take the battle out of the court into the nation, to raise the standard of loyal rebellion as the only way left to them if they were to succeed in reversing the defeats suffered at court and in parliament, and in forcing the King to change his policy'.[7]

According to his interpretation it was Henry's attempt to end his marriage to Catherine of Aragon that started the problems. These were then exacerbated by the centralising policy of the king that was undermining the strong feudal ties in the north. The men who led the rising had lost out in the recent religious and political changes to men such as Thomas Cromwell and Richard Riche. They felt that the court was now dominated by the Boleyn faction and other men of low birth, such as Cromwell and Riche, who had no right to be advising the king on matters of policy – that should be reserved for those of noble status. This view is supported by an examination of the Pilgrims' Ballad that concludes with following comment:

1   Cromwell, Cranmer, and Riche
    As all three are the same
    As some men teach
    God amend their ways
5   And that Aske may,
    Without delay,
    Here make a stay
    And achieve his aims.

These three men were seen as being responsible for the unpopular religious policies of the 1530s and now appeared to have a monopoly of court patronage to the exclusion of others.

In order to evaluate this view we must ask, who were those who were losing out? According to Elton's interpretation, they were the supporters of the king's first wife, Catherine of Aragon. This is clearly illustrated in the case of Hussey. He had been Princess Mary's chamberlain and had lost his office and his wife was imprisoned in the Tower when he was alleged to have encouraged Mary to resist Cromwell's demands that she fully accept the Royal Supremacy. A similar picture emerges of Aske, Darcy and Constable; they were all members of what has been termed the Aragonese faction. There is even evidence that Hussey and Darcy had been in conversation with the Imperial Ambassador and had contemplated resorting to arms as early as 1534 in order to try to reverse their declining fortunes.

There is certainly sufficient evidence to suggest that they had a motive for rising. As the power of central government in London grew under Cromwell, so their influence in politics declined. It appeared as if all decisions were being made in the capital and that the north was being excluded: hence their call for a parliament in the north. It is also true that many northern families had done badly in recent times, and it is interesting to note that one of the few families that had done well, the Cliffords, remained loyal in defending Skipton, Carlisle and Berwick throughout the rising. On the other hand, the major family of the north, the Percies, had suffered a considerable loss of prestige. The king had put a great deal of pressure on Henry Percy to name the king as his sole heir, and as a result disinherit Thomas Percy of the Percy estates. It should therefore come as no surprise to discover that the disinherited brothers played a large part in the rising. In fact every council of the rising had at least one Percy in it and Aske himself had links with the Percy family. These men realised that only a reversal of recent changes would restore their fortunes, and this is shown in the Pontefract Articles:

> We humbly beg our most powerful sovereign lord that the Lady Mary may be made legitimate and the former statute annulled.

The restoration of Mary to the succession would represent a triumph for the conservative faction and their restoration to political predominance as it would require the removal of the Boleyn faction and all they represented.

Although it may be easy to show that this group had motives for rising, we must also be able to show that they were the leaders of the rising and that they rose for political reasons. Darcy's actions at Pontefract Castle suggest that they had been preparing to rise. The surrender of the castle was too easy and the sudden appearance of the Pilgrims' badges suggests that the rising was not spontaneous but planned. This argument is supported by the earlier comments made to the Imperial ambassador. However, there are arguments against such a view. A detailed examination of some northern families reveals some contradictory interpretations. Some of the most active gentry in the rising had no connections with the Percy family and some actually had grievances against them. Moreover, if it was a rising by the excluded northern families, why didn't the Westmorland family play a role? And Lord Dacre, who had nearly been charged with treason in 1534, had nothing to do with the rising.

e) Conclusion

There has been a great deal of simplification in the assessment of the causes of the rising. Many historians have explained the rising as being due to one cause, but this ignores its real character and the very complex nature of the protest. It was, after all, a rising that involved a wide range of social movements and groups, each with their own grievances, and this was reflected in the demands made. It must also be remembered that the rising was actually a series of regional revolts each with its own particular emphasis. Perhaps it is best seen as a complex inter-reaction of factors that should include religion, the personal dislike of Cromwell and his policies, the dislike of paying taxes, bad harvests and rumours. A careful examination of the demands of the pilgrims shows that virtually any interpretation can be supported – hence the wide range of interpretations that historians have produced. In order to overcome this problem historians have asked whose revolt was it, believing that if they can answer this question they will be able to identify the cause of the rising. However, this has still failed to produce a consensus as to whether it was a rising of the commons aided by the gentry, or of the gentry assisted by the lower orders. What can be said with certainty is that the whole of northern society was out of joint and that a remedy was needed. This is the only plausible explanation for a rising that involved so many people from such a wide range of social groups. In many ways they reverted back to the only form of protest known to them, but on the other hand it was unique in that it was conceived as a pilgrimage.

5 The 1537 Rising

At Doncaster the Pilgrims appeared to have achieved many of

KEY ISSUE What was the significance of the Rising?

their aims, but Henry was waiting for his opportunity to exact revenge. The chance came in the winter of 1537. The Duke of Norfolk had spent longer in London with the king than expected and some leading northern gentlemen had been summoned to the capital, creating the impression that Henry was not going to keep his word and was plotting revenge. The commons felt betrayed as nothing concrete had happened despite the king's promises and Aske was no longer able to impose his authority on the area. The commons began to rise in January under Sir Francis Bigod. Their plan was to capture Hull and Scarborough, but this failed. Bigod was soon captured in Cumberland, but here the commons now mustered on their own initiative. This was Henry's chance and Norfolk made no mistake; the rebels were defeated in an attack at Carlisle. Martial law was declared and 74 were hanged at Carlisle. Meanwhile gentry leaders were rounded up and taken to London for trial and just over another 100 lost their lives. Given the scale of the risings this number is very low, but Henry sent out a very clear message: he expected obedience and loyalty. It was the ruling class who paid with their lives as among those executed were Darcy, Aske, Hussey and leaders of the various Pilgrim hosts.

But we must not just see this as a continuation of the Pilgrimage. In particular, the leadership was very different. Bigod was not a catholic, but instead an enthusiastic evangelical. He realised that Henry had no intention of keeping his word and was therefore determined to start a new rising to ensure that the area's grievances were taken seriously. His plan involved the capture of the Duke of Norfolk so that he could be used as an intermediary with the government until the grievances were corrected.

Although the rising was a disaster it sent a clear message to the government in London and resulted in Henry building up his own interest in the north and reorganising the Council of the North so as to include those who had an understanding of the area, some of whom had even been in the Pilgrimage. This, and the avoidance of further pressures and changes, ensured that the last years saw no more serious unrest; and in 1549, when the west country rose against the religious changes (see pages 52–5), the north remained quiet.

6 The Significance of the Pilgrimage of Grace

> **KEY ISSUE** Was the Pilgrimage of Grace a failure or did it change royal policy?

For many years the Pilgrimage of Grace was seen as a failure. It was very easy to understand this explanation. The rebels had apparently failed in their aims and with their slaughter at Carlisle in February 1537, and subsequent retributions, a clear warning had been sent out to all would-be trouble-makers across the land. At the same time they had failed to stop the Dissolution of the Monasteries; in fact the remainder of the great religious houses would be closed by 1540. The main target of their complaint, Thomas Cromwell, was still in power, and political power was still firmly based in London as the promised parliament in the north never met.

Given these failings it is surely very difficult to see the pilgrimage as anything but a failure. However, recent work by Michael Bush suggests a very different story. He views the pilgrimage as a success and believes that it achieved many of its aims. The greatest success that the rebels had was in raising such a large force. This was much larger than any other Tudor rebellion and could easily have defeated the royal forces had it so wished, but that was never the aim of the leadership. The force was there to intimidate and pressurise the king. Without doubt the sheer scale of the rising must have acted as a warning. At a time when there was no other way to register protest, the pilgrimage represents large-scale dissatisfaction with the regime. The large numbers raised also enabled the pilgrims to put pressure on the king at a number of crucial moments. It was the pilgrims who chose to reach a negotiated settlement in both October and December. The settlement represented a massive climb-down for the government; they had suggested the second meeting because they did not have the force to challenge the rebels. The government was forced to allow a free and general pardon for all those who had taken part. There were no exceptions and the king was unable to apprehend the ring-leaders.

There were also specific successes for the pilgrims. They had secured the promise of a free parliament in the north and a promise that until it met nothing would be done to implement the policies to which the rebels objected. This meant that the smaller monasteries the pilgrims had restored were allowed to stand, much against the wishes of the king. At the same time further changes in the government's religious policy followed. The most obvious sign of change was the appearance of the Bishops' Book in 1537. This restored many conservative practices. It recognised the four lost sacraments that had been absent from the Ten Articles of 1536. There was also an attack on those most protestant of practices, radical preaching and clerical marriage. There certainly appeared to be the real prospect of a conservative reaction and it can be argued that any intended religious revolution had to be postponed until Edward VI's reign.

However, it was not just in religious matters that the pilgrims were successful. They stopped the collection of the subsidy and made it clear that any further financial changes would be unacceptable. Any further moves towards a Tudor revolution in government were abandoned. This may also have weakened the position of the rebels' major cause of complaint, Thomas Cromwell. Although he did not immediately fall from power, the two policies with which he was most closely associated, administrative reform and religious innovation, were abandoned.

Lastly, it is important not to forget that some of the rebels had specific agrarian grievances. Those from Cumberland and Westmorland had objected to the increase in entry fines, but this issue was now resolved in favour of the rebels with the cost being fixed at twice the rent. This was exactly the amount demanded by the rebels in the December petition.

The government had been pressured into accepting the demands of the pilgrims. As Michael Bush concluded in his study, 'in these respects, then, the formation of the pilgrim armies in October 1536 has to be appreciated not only as a spectacular achievement in itself but also as a major influence upon religious, political, fiscal and agrarian changes of the time'.[8]

References

1 J.J. Scarisbrick, *Henry VIII* (Pelican, 1971), p. 187.
2 N.R. Fellows, The Pilgrimage of Grace, in *History Review*, September 2000.
3 G.R. Elton, Politics and the Pilgrimage of Grace, in *After the Reformation: Essays in honour of J.H. Hexter* (University of Pennsylvania Press, 1980), p. 203.
4 John Guy, *Tudor England*, p. 151.
5 Christopher Haigh, *Reformation and Resistance in Tudor Lancashire* (CUP, 1975), pp. 118–138.
6 A.G. Dickens, *The English Reformation* (Fontana, 1967), p. 182.
7 G.R. Elton, *Reform and Reformation* (Edward Arnold, 1977), p. 267.
8 M.L. Bush, *The Pilgrimage of Grace* (Manchester University Press, 1996), p. 417.

Summary Diagram
The Pilgrimage of Grace: The most serious challenge?

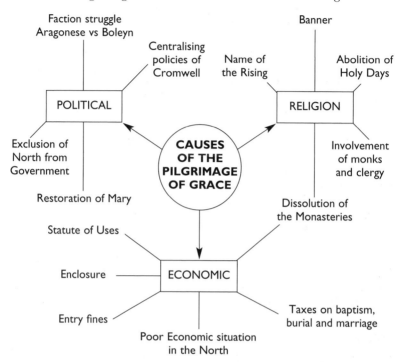

Was the Pilgrimage a failure? A balance sheet

FAILURE	SUCCESS
Dissolution Continues 1539–40	
Cromwell survives	Cromwell falls 1540
Massacre at Carlisle 1537	Pardon 1536
Parliament in north never meets	Promise of Parliament in the north
Reformation continues under Edward VI	Delays Reformation
	Scale of the Rising
	Entry fines
	Subsidy stopped

Read the extracts from the Pontefract Articles on page 39 and from the Pilgrims' Ballad on page 38, and answer the following questions.

a) Explain the reference to 'the Lady Mary may be made legitimate'. (*10 marks*)

b) How reliable is the Pilgrims' Ballad as a source of information for the causes of the Pilgrimage of Grace? (*20 marks*)

c) 'Religion was the prime cause of the Pilgrimage of Grace'. Using the sources and your own knowledge how far is this an accurate assessment of the causes of the Pilgrimage of the Grace? (*60 marks*)

All the examination boards set document papers at either AS or A2. Their purpose is to test your understanding of contemporary sources or of the views of historians. The questions in this section are all based around contemporary extracts on one particular rebellion, but very often the coverage will be much wider and you may be given sources on different rebellions to compare.

The first question tests your understanding or comprehension of a particular source. Although there are ten marks available you need not write more than a short paragraph. It is therefore important that you get to the focus of the extract and explain accurately any terms or concepts. This will require you to use your own knowledge, in this instance on the Act declaring Mary illegitimate. You should be able to name the act and then explain why this was important to the Pilgrims.

The second question concerns the reliability of a source. There are two ways that this should be done. Firstly consider who wrote the source, why it was written and the words used to see if there is any-thing that would make it either reliable or unreliable. However, if you are looking for top marks you should test what the source says against your own knowledge. Is there anything that you know that either agrees or disagrees with what is said in the source? In this question you would score about half marks for using just the source and the other marks would be available for the use of your own knowledge.

The last question carries a large number of marks and requires a lengthy answer. It is almost the equivalent of an essay and it is important in an examination that you leave enough time to do yourself justice on a question of this type. The question states that you should use all the sources and your own knowledge: this is important if you want to achieve high marks. The examiners would expect about half of the answer to be drawn from the sources and half from your own knowledge. You need to consider what the sources say were the causes and whether you can trust their assess-ment. Having done that, you should bring in your own knowledge as to the causes and perhaps challenge what the sources say were the causes. In this instance you could also mention the struggle of the Aragonese faction to regain influence; credit would be gained if you explained that this was Elton's interpretation. If you use only the sources or your own knowledge you would score under half marks, so it is important to read the question carefully before you start writing!

Now apply these skills to the following source-based questions:

1. The Lincolnshire rising

Read Nicholas Leche's statement about the Lincolnshire rising on page 28.

a) How reliable is this source as an explanation of the behaviour of the gentry during the Lincolnshire rising? (20 marks)

Now look at the pictures of Louth church on page 29 and the Pilgrim's banner on page 34.

b) Why were the people of Louth prepared to spend money on the new steeple for their church? (5 marks)
c) How far does this help us to understand why there was a rising in Lincolnshire in 1536? (10 marks)
d) What can we learn about the causes of the Pilgrimage of Grace from the badge? (10 marks)
e) To what extent do these sources indicate that opposition to Henry VIII in 1536 was primarily for religious reasons? (25 marks)

4 Class Warfare and Anarchy: The Reign of Edward VI

POINTS TO CONSIDER

This chapter deals with the two major rebellions of Edward's reign. However, it places them in the wider context of the long- and short-term changes that had taken place. You need to decide whether the rebellions were the result of the long-term changes or whether they were a response to specific changes in government policy under Edward. A major issue for you to consider is how far the revolts were class-based and whether the monarchy was ever seriously challenged.

KEY DATES

1540s		Rapid population growth, inflation and rising unemployment.
1547	Jan	Death of Henry VIII.
	Feb	Edward Seymour created Duke of Somerset and Lord Protector.
	Sep	Invasion of Scotland.
1548		Proclamation to remove images from churches.
		Dissolution of the Chantries.
	April	Murder of William Body at Helston, Cornwall.
	June	Enclosure Commission to enforce existing laws.
1549		Tax on Sheep and Cloth.
		More Enclosure Commissions.
	Jan	Act of Uniformity and Book of Common Prayer.
	June	Introduction of First Prayer Book.
		Western or Prayer Book Rebellion.
	July	Ket's Rebellion in East Anglia.
	Oct	Fall of Somerset.
		Poor harvest.

1 Introduction

Although the concept of a mid-Tudor crisis has been challenged over recent years, it is difficult to escape the fact that the years 1547–1553 saw a large number of disturbances. In particular, 1549 saw two serious rebellions and numerous other minor disturbances, which some historians believe brought England close to class war.[1]

There were tensions in both town and countryside as economic problems reached new levels of intensity. Changes in central government and religion had also loosened loyalty to the regime so that those discontented by the hard times were ready recruits for those who wished to overturn Tudor rule.

2 The Social and Economic Context

> **KEY ISSUES** Was there an underlying economic crisis in mid-Tudor society and, if so, how far did it contribute to the unrest of the period?

For the first time since the Black Death of the fourteenth century the population of England was rising steadily and from about 1525 it appears that the rise was more rapid. It is very difficult to be precise about this growth as there is no reliable statistical information. However, it would appear that it had risen from about 2.3 million in 1525 to 3 million by 1551.[2] Although this rise was nowhere near as significant as that of the eighteenth century it did contribute to the problems of Edward's reign and would be an issue in the later sixteenth century. There is evidence that people were marrying at an earlier age and therefore the average family size was rising. Meanwhile there was an increase in the 'dependency ratio' as there were an increasing number of children who did not contribute to the productivity of the nation, but who were consumers of food. Although the population rise helped to stimulate industrial demand and production was able to respond accordingly, this was less true of agriculture. Here demand outstripped supply and resulted in a period of rapid price rises. The population growth also created other problems. Jobs were created by the growing industrial demand, but in times of slump it meant that workers became unemployed and, lacking any other form of income, they became either dependent upon charity and poor relief or vagrants who were seen as a threat to law and order.

Agricultural production struggled to keep pace with the growing population. In times of good harvests this was less of a problem, but when harvests were poor the problem was very serious. Unfortunately for the government a significant number of harvests in the period 1540–59 were deficient, putting further pressure on food supplies. It was very difficult to increase productivity in the short term given the lack of scientific measures available to farmers. The only available measure was to increase the amount of land under the plough, but this frequently meant bringing marginal land under cultivation where returns were poor. At the same time the demand for cloth grew and farmers saw that there was a very lucrative market available to them in sheep farming. This required less labour, but also encouraged enclosure, particularly of common land. It was the peasants who lost out by this. Fewer labourers were required to work the land as it takes less labour to look after a flock of sheep than it does to till the soil. Secondly the peasants were dependent upon the common land to graze their flocks and supplement their diets through catching rabbits or gathering the berries. It is therefore hardly surprising that many of the disturbances of this period were protests against enclosure. There were even worse problems in the towns. The lack of an internal transport system meant that it was very difficult to supply the urban areas and a local harvest failure soon created problems for the local authorities. Starvation in either the towns or countryside could soon turn into desperate violence and a challenge to either local or central government.

The rising population was also a factor in the price rise of the mid and late sixteenth century. Although there is still much debate about the precise causes, what is clear is the impact that it had. The inability of the agricultural sector to keep pace with population growth resulted in inflation, particularly in food prices, throughout the sixteenth century and on an unprecedented scale. However, as the chart below shows, this rise was even worse in the mid-Tudor period. This corresponds with the period of Henry VIII's and Edward VI's wars against both France and Scotland. In order to finance military activities the government debased the coinage by reducing the amount of silver content. This simply put more money into circulation and that inevitably had an impact on prices as the amount of food available did not rise.

The chart shows that prices had more than doubled over the first half of the sixteenth century, and the situation was even worse for grain prices. This had important consequences as bread was the staple diet of the masses, and the peasantry found themselves frequently in a state of poverty. As all the available evidence also suggests that the rise in wages was even slower, it resulted in a considerable fall in living standards.

The fall in the standard of living resulted in a rise in the number of poor. Estimates have suggested that about half the population were unable to support themselves. The dissolution of the monasteries and enclosure had already increased the number of poor people. However, the size of the problem increased at times of harvest failure and during depressions in the cloth trade, both of which were serious

Prices for the Years 1500–1550
(The figures are based on an index, where 1508=100)

Year	Index	Year	Index
1500	94	1540	158
1508	100	1545	191
1520	137	1546	248
1530	169	1549	214

issues in mid-Tudor England. Poverty was a particular cause of concern in towns because of the size of the problem and the concentration of large numbers of vagrants who were perceived to be a threat to law and order. It was a serious issue because many of the poor turned to crime, whilst others became beggars. This latter group often included former soldiers and sailors who were often armed. Without a police force, the government was often left to take draconian measures to try to ensure that these vagabonds did not become involved in insurrection. This culminated during Edward VI's reign in the notorious 1547 Act, which condemned vagrants to slavery for two years for a first offence and life for any subsequent misdemeanour. The passage of such a savage act is clear evidence of the government's concern at a growing problem. It was obvious that earlier legislation was not working and that given the scale of the economic problems in mid Tudor England a clear warning was necessary to discourage the peasantry and prevent the likelihood of riots.

3 The Religious Context

> **KEY ISSUE** How far had the religious changes of Henry VIII undermined society?

The religious changes of Henry's reign had left a confused situation. Many of the old catholic practices still remained. The sacraments were untouched, clerical marriage was forbidden and the old mass was still common practice. However, the monastic orders had gone, the royal supremacy had removed papal authority, and the vernacular Bible and services in English gave many access to the word of God. More importantly the changes had undermined church authority. The sacrificial role of the parish priest had been reduced with the destruction of rood screens lessening their elevated status, whilst the growth in the belief in justification by faith challenged their role as the link between man and God. At the same time the peasantry were being taught that charity and good works did not shorten their time in purgatory. Moreover, the dissolution of the monasteries implied that purgatory might not even exist. Traditional religious practices that still satisfied the majority of the population had been undermined.

More importantly for the government the religious changes had dismantled one element of traditional authority. The church had traditionally helped to underpin the hierarchical nature of society, but the attack on the role of priests, monks and nuns had left a void in local society and removed one of the ties that bound society together. With the decline in the sacerdotal and sacramental role of the priest he lost much respect and could no longer be relied upon to impose order from the pulpit. As a result one of the long-standing props of the state had been called into question. The religious innovations had also caused changes in people's perspective and in communal activities. Accessibility to the Bible had made new ideas available to the masses and further challenged fundamental acceptance about the role of the individual within society.

4 Short-term Problems: The Reign of Edward VI

> **KEY ISSUE** How were the problems of the early years of Edward's reign responsible for the unrest of 1549?

a) The Minority

The last years of Henry's reign had witnessed an intense faction struggle as it became obvious that the king would die before his son was of age. At stake was control of the government. The struggle was between the Seymour faction, led by the Earl of Hertford (later the Duke of Somerset), and the Norfolk faction. By the end of Henry's reign Hertford had been able to secure power as Protector and was in a position to reward his supporters. However, there was no guarantee that the Protectorship would be accepted. There were fears of conflict and the clergy had to be ordered to preach obedience from the pulpit. Somerset's difficulties were added to as he lacked the trappings of royal authority. He could not fall back on the claim that he was God's anointed, whilst unpopularity in his policies could easily lead to his position being challenged.

This factional struggle had an increased intensity as it was mirrored by a religious divide in the royal council. Whoever controlled the boy king would be able to determine the religious direction of the country. Moreover, as religious loyalty and the succession became intertwined, the hope for political stability became even less. Although it was not inevitable that a minority would create problems, regencies had ruined the rule of earlier monarchs. The reigns of Henry III and Henry VI had led to conflict among councillors, whilst Richard II had been deposed and Edward V murdered.

b) Religion

The religious position at the end of Henry's reign was confused. However, the triumph of the Seymour faction appeared to ensure a protestant victory. Edward was brought up by protestant tutors and was himself a firm supporter of the reformed religion. Thomas Cranmer had survived all the conservative attacks against him and was now in a position to implement change. By the start of 1549 it was apparent that England had made at least a cautious move towards protestantism. This was evident with the smashing of images, destruction of wall paintings and the breaking of stained glass windows. Proclamations had to be issued in London to restrain the crowds and prevent the iconoclasm turning into open riot. However, this was just the start; these attacks were followed by the dissolution of chantries, where masses had been sung for the souls of the dead. This appeared to complete the process begun by Henry with his attack on monasteries. Not only had the visual appearance of churches changed, but also the doctrinal position moved closer to protestantism. The Prayer Book of 1549 and Act of Uniformity appeared to confirm this as they denied the real presence and affirmed that the communion service was only commemorative. The ambiguity that was present with the retention of altars and traditional vestments did not do enough to satisfy many conservatives, whilst it did not go far enough for the radicals.

Despite a growing belief on the continent that the people should accept the religion of the ruler, this was undermined in England by Edward's youth. The attacks on the church under both Henry and Edward had done much to undermine its credibility and confidence in the official doctrine was missing. Most of the country was still conservative in its religious outlook and it is hardly surprising that these changes were, at least in part, the cause of unrest or that complaints about the religious direction figured prominently among the grievances of the Western rebels in 1549.

c) Social Problems

There were already many long-term social and economic issues facing the new government. However, their attitude and policies often served to make matters worse. In order to try to improve his own position Protector Somerset continued the war with Scotland, hoping for the success that would secure his position. This never came, but it did ensure that the policy of debasement was continued and that inflation rose even faster. This determination to continue the Scottish war may also explain Somerset's decision to tackle the issue of enclosure.[3] Many contemporaries believed that the greed of landowners, who were enclosing land and thereby depriving the peasantry of work and reducing the amount of food grown, was the primary cause of inflation. In this atmosphere it was vital that something be done if the government was to avoid trouble. Therefore, in both 1548 and 1549, commissioners were appointed to investigate enclosure. This was seen as even more important when the harvest of 1548 was poor. However, these commissions achieved nothing practical as landowners objected to the interference and blocked attempts in parliament to limit enclosure. Somerset then issued a proclamation to force landowners to reverse their enclosure. This had two effects. Firstly, landowners and other nobles, upon whom Somerset relied for support, were not pleased with him, believing that he was showing too much sympathy for the lower orders. Secondly, the lower orders perceived that in the Protector they had a champion and that with others, such as Bishop Latimer, preaching against the greed of landowners, they might at last have support among the government. Therefore, when the government failed in their actions, many of the commons may have been encouraged to take the law into their own hands and pull down the enclosures themselves. It is therefore hardly surprising that many of the riots and rebellions of 1549 had enclosure as a cause.

5 The Western Rebellion

> **KEY ISSUE** Was the Western Rebellion caused by the religious changes or was the rising the result of social conflict?

a) The events

The Western Rebellion is also known as the Prayer Book rising and an examination of events before it occurred suggests that this is an accurate description. There had already been discontent in Cornwall in 1547 when William Body, a local archdeacon and known protestant sympathiser, had been attacked. In 1548 he had returned to the area in order to supervise the destruction of images and was murdered. Finally, in 1549, many of the peasants in Cornwall had risen against the imposition of the Act of Uniformity and set up camp at Bodmin.

However, the rising in Cornwall was only the prelude to a much larger event in Devon. The rising started at Sampford Courtenay on Whit Monday when the locals objected to the use of the new Prayer Book and insisted that the priest say Mass according to the old style. By June 20 the rebels from Devon and Cornwall had joined forces at Crediton, where they were offered a pardon if they would disperse. However, this offer was rejected and the rebels proceeded to set up camp at Clyst St. Mary, near Exeter. When negotiations again failed the rebel army of some 6,000 began to beseige Exeter. Meanwhile Lord Russell had been sent to put the rising down. He had been delayed because he had to deal with other outbreaks of unrest in Oxfordshire, but once he did arrive the rebels forces were destroyed and some 4,000 killed.

b) The demands of the rebels

The rebels' demands were drawn up by the clergy. Therefore, it is hardly surprising that they illustrate a strong sense of religious conservatism.

They complained about the religious changes that they thought were taking place in baptism and confirmation. The rebels also wanted the restoration of many of the old religious practices, hence

Item we will have the Laws of our Sovereign Lord King Henry VIII concerning the Six Articles, to be in use again, as they were during his reign.

Item we will have the mass in Latin, as it was before, and celebrated by the priest without any man or woman communicating with him ...

Item we will have holy bread and holy water every Sunday, palms and ashes at the accustomed times, Images set up again in every church ...

Item we will not receive the new service because it is like a Christmas game, but we will have our old service of Matins, mass, Evensong and procession in Latin not in English ...

Item we will have every preacher in his sermon, and every priest at mass, pray individually for the souls in purgatory, as our forefathers did ...

12. Item we think it is right that because Lord Cardinal Pole is of the king's blood, he should not only have a free pardon, but also be sent for from Rome, and be promoted to be first or second in the king's council ...

Item we will that half the abbey and chantry lands, in every man's possession, however he came by them, be given again to two places, where two of the chief abbeys used to be ...

article two's call for the restoration of the Six Articles. This would undermine all the work of the Edwardian reformation (outlined on pages 50–1). There was a strong desire for much of the ceremony and ritual of catholicism – hence the rebels' desire to have the mass in Latin, even though they did not understand it, and the restoration of images. They also wanted the return of many old traditions, such as holy bread and water. There was also a wish to see traditional doctrine brought back as they asserted a belief in both transubstantiation and purgatory. Most clearly of all the demands was an attack on protestantism. The rebels attacked communion in both kinds and the new Prayer Book, which was seen as symbolic of the new religion.

However, although religious grievances dominated the demands there are indications of other complaints. Article 12 demands the return of Pole. But, what is interesting is that the request is for him to return, not as a Cardinal, but as a member of the king's council. The rebels probably hoped to be able to use him as their political leader. Perhaps the rebels believed that if they could get a religious conservative on to the council then their grievances would be listened to, or that he could reverse the changes that Somerset had introduced. Pole also had Yorkist connections and it is possible that, by demanding a political role for him, they were hoping to see the crown revert to the

Yorkists. If this was the case it shows that the Tudor succession was still not accepted by everyone. The rebels also called for Richard Crispin and John Moreman to be released so that they could preach again in the west. Although they appear to be demanding the return of two clerics, whose religious views coincided with their own, there was also a political significance to this request. Moreman had opposed Henry's divorce from Catherine and Crispin had served as Chaplain to Courtenay. Therefore it could be argued that the rising raised again the spectre of the White Rose of the Yorkists, as great a worry for Somerset as it had been for Henry.

Despite the economic and social grievances of the time it is surprising that the demands do not reflect these concerns. Although there is evidence that the rebels condemned the new sheep tax, which if applied would hit them hard, it does not appear in their final list of grievances. However, the action of the rebels does suggest that social tensions were an important factor in the rising.

c) The actions of the rebels

The first major challenge to the primacy of religion as a cause of the rising came in 1900 from A.F. Pollard, who suggested that social issues were at the core of the rising. Throughout the rebellion the behaviour of the rebels appears to make it clear that the gentry were their enemies. The Cornish rebels had started by attacking and robbing the gentry at St. Michael's Mount and at Bodmin they had shouted 'Kill the Gentlemen'. Meanwhile, in Devon the rebels had killed William Hellyons, the only member of the gentry class who was brave enough to resist them. They attacked Trematon Castle, plundered it and put its owner in gaol.

However, it was not just the rebels who carried out acts of class warfare. Government forces set fire to part of the rebels' defences at Crediton, causing one historian to note that 'the charred barns and houses stood as grim reminders of the widening cleavage between the landowning gentry and the masses of working men and women'.[4]

This interpretation is also supported by the actions of the city government during the siege of Exeter. Following the failure of negotiations the rebels were able to create a food shortage within the city and to cut its water supply. These actions added to the tensions and there was near rioting within the city. The mayor and other officials feared that the poor would hand over the city to the rebels. In order to try to prevent this some of the more wealthy citizens organised a continual guard, provided poor relief, sold firewood cheaply and distributed food at either a low cost or free to the poorer elements within the city. This was a success and the mayor was able to unite the town. However, their view of the rebels outside the walls as 'refuse, scum, and the rascals of the whole county' is further evidence of the divide that was apparent in local society.

A closer examination of the rebel demands may also support this view. Both articles 13 and 14 hint at tensions within west-country society. The rebels wanted to limit the number of servants that the gentry could employ and they also called for the restoration of some monastic lands. This would have hit the gentry as they were the very group who had gained from the dissolution and had bought up former monastic estates. In fact, it is possible to suggest that there is a link between the rebels' religious grievances and their attack upon the gentry: it was after all the gentry who had gained from the Reformation. They had also been responsible for the implementation of the unpopular religious policy. Therefore, the rebellion gave the peasantry an opportunity to attack both causes of their dissatisfaction: the religious policy of Somerset and the failings of the gentry.

Contemporary commentators agreed that social issues played an important role in the rising. Even the leader of the royal army sent against the rebels drew attention to the exploitation of the commons by the nobility who raised rents excessively. In the past the nobility had cared for their tenants, particularly in times of crises. But the concept of 'good lordship', where the commons received fair rents, employment, protection and generosity from their superiors, had disappeared. This concept may always have been a myth, but what is clear is that, while it had once existed in the minds of many of the peasantry, it had gone by the mid-sixteenth century. As a consequence, they were subject to ever increasing burdens. Therefore, when trouble broke out the gentry, the traditional keepers of law and order, were not only unable to keep the peace but were the targets of the rising.

6 Ket's Rebellion

> **KEY ISSUES** Was Ket's rebellion just an anti-enclosure riot, or was it the result of class conflict?

a) The events

The major disturbance in East Anglia took its name from its leader Robert Ket. The rising had started as an attack on enclosure with riots at the Norfolk towns of Attleborough and Wymondham. In particular the rioters were angry with a local lawyer, Sir John Flowerdew, who had been putting up fences and had bought the local abbey church which he was now pulling down. Flowerdew was also involved in a land dispute with Ket and tried to turn the rioters against him. However, Ket was able to seize the initiative, assume leadership and turn the rebels against Flowerdew's land. Ket had soon gathered a force of some 16,000 men and they proceeded towards Norwich, setting up camp at Mousehold Heath on the outskirts. The local authorities were unable to disperse the force and it was left to the royal herald to offer the rebels a pardon to disperse. Unfortunately for the authorities, this had the opposite effect and the rebels seized Norwich. With the second city of England in rebel hands the government was forced to act and so sent the Marquis of Northampton with 14,000 troops against the rebels. Northampton was able to take the city, but was forced to abandon it the next day. The government now sent Dudley, Earl of Warwick, against the rebels. He brought the rebels to battle at Dussindale, just outside Norwich, where over 3,000 rebels were killed. Ket was captured and hanged for sedition.

b) The Demands of the Rebels

The rebels drew up a list of 29 articles. These demands show that the causes of the rising were wide ranging and only one article refers specifically to enclosure.

Despite the wide variety of demands, there were a number of areas of life that received particular attention. Enclosure was just one among many agricultural demands made by the rebels, and many of these complaints concerned particular farming practices in certain

Articles of the Norfolk Rebels 1549

3. We pray your grace that no lord of the manor encloses the common land.

5. We pray that Reed ground and meadow ground are the same rent as they were in the first year of King Henry VII.

8. We pray that priests or vicars that are unable to preach and set forth the word of God to their parishioners may be removed from their benefice and the parishioners choose another ...

10. We pray that no man under the status of knight or esquire keep a dovecotes, unless it was an ancient custom.

14. We pray that copyhold land that has an unreasonable rent is let at the same rent as it was in the first year of King Henry VII ...

16. We pray that all bond men may be made free for God made everyone free with his precious blood shedding.

19. We pray that the poor mariners or fisherman have all the profits of their fishing

28. We pray that those local officials who have offended the commons, and where it has been proved by the complaints of the poor commons, give 4d to these poor men for every day they have remained there.

29. We pray that no lord, knight, esquire, or gentlemen graze or feed any bullocks or sheep if he has an income of £40 per year from his lands, unless it is for the provision of his house.

areas of East Anglia. The first demand expressed concern about saffron, a valuable crop grown in the area around Saffron Walden. Meanwhile, demand 29 expressed anger about the gentry's manipulation of the foldcourse system used in Norfolk and North West Suffolk. According to this custom the gentry had the right to graze their sheep on the peasants' fallow and unsown land. The gentry had been extending the length of time in the year that they could use this right by lengthening the stubble period and allowing their sheep to wander over winter corn. The gentry had also been overstocking the common land, as is suggested in the third demand, particularly in the heavy soil areas of central East Anglia. It was in this region that enclosure was an issue and there is evidence of fences being thrown down. However, farming in East Anglia also included fishing as many peasants relied upon this to supplement their diets. The rebels wanted rivers to be open to all for fishing and in article 19 made demands about the coastal fishing industry.

Closely linked to the agricultural demands were those concerning the rents on land. The peasants were already under pressure from gentry encroachment on to common land and now they were also put under increasing financial pressure. In a period of rising prices landlords were looking to recoup their losses by increasing rents in a variety of ways. Articles 5 and 14 are just two of the demands that call for rents to be at the level they were under Henry VII when economic conditions were more favourable. These demands suggest that perhaps the harsh economic conditions of 1549 were a major cause of the unrest.

The rebels also had religious grievances, but unlike the Western Rebellion these demands were decidedly protestant. They supported the religious changes and often wanted them to go further. Article 8 is concerned about poor clerical standards and called for the removal of incompetent priests who were unable to preach. This article looked forward to Elizabeth's reign when ministers who taught and preached regularly were in demand. The rebels' actions at Mousehold Heath appear to support this as they brought in ministers who were able to preach and used the new Prayer Book. Later articles also expressed concern about non-resident clergy and the need for priests to teach children the basic Christian beliefs.

However, perhaps the greatest number of complaints concerned the social structure and local government in the region. The demands suggest that there had been a breakdown in trust between the governing class and those just below on the social ladder. We have already seen complaints against the nobility and gentry as landlords, but there were also grievances against them as officers of local government. In particular they criticised officers of the Court of Wards: the feodary and escheator. But when it is realised that Flowerdew was the escheator, such antagonism is easily understood. Perhaps the greatest rebuke to local government officers is shown in article 28 where the rebels demand that each officer who has offended them pay them 4d for every day they are assembled. The rebels also accepted the privileges of the gentry. This is shown in their concern about the right to keep doves and rabbits by those under a certain rank. However, if the gentry had certain privileges, they also had certain duties and were expected to preserve traditional social boundaries.

The demands appear to indicate a socially conservative peasantry. Even the deferential opening of each demand appears to support this view. However, despite their language it is important not to be misled by their conservatism. In their demands this is shown most clearly by article 16, where Ket appears to be showing concern for the poor. Although serfdom had largely disappeared from England it had been retained on some of the Howard's estates in Norfolk. With their demise in 1547 this was the ideal time to end the process and to establish a commonwealth of free men.

If Ket's demands were to be achieved, they required sweeping action from the government. However, the rebels also put forward suggestions as to how this could be achieved. In the past local government had been in the hands of the gentry, power would now be put in the hands of the people. Their actions set out to show that this would work.

c) The actions of the Rebels

Some historians have explained the events of 1549 in terms of class conflict. According to this interpretation the social and economic changes that were outlined in Section 2 had created antagonism between the governing classes and the lower orders. As the rich got richer, through the exploitation of rents and other feudal dues, so the poor got poorer. The lower orders reacted by establishing an alternative system, whereby they excluded the gentry and tried to re-establish an imaginary past where all knew their place. How far do the actions of the rebels support this interpretation?

The rebels' actions certainly showed that they wanted to establish an alternative system of local government. In establishing a series of camps at centres associated with local government, such as Norwich, Ipswich and Downham Market, they were making a clear statement that they did not want mob rule. From the camp at Mousehold Heath Ket issued commissions and writs, in the same form as the Crown purveyor, to some of the rebels to bring in food and drink from the local area. Once again this was designed to give the appearance of authority and show that, although they were perceived as the lower orders, they were able to behave without the leadership of the gentry.

The camps were used to administer justice, suggesting that not only did the rebels have a concern for law and order but that they were keen to show that they could maintain discipline, something that the traditional rulers had failed to achieve. At Mousehold gentlemen were brought before Ket and were put on trial under the 'old oak' or 'the tree of Reformation'. However, the trials also show that there was social tension in society. This is made clear by the comments of a contemporary commentator:

1   those gentlemen they captured they brought to the tree of Reformation where they asked the people what they wanted to do with them: some cried hang them and some kill them. Some, who were unable to hear shouted like the rest and when asked why they did that, answered that
5   they copied their fellows. They also pushed their weapons into the gentlemen in order to kill some of those brought to them, and they did this with such malice that one Mr. Wharton, who was being guarded by a line of men on both sides all the way from the tree to the city, was pricked with their spears and other weapons on purpose to kill him ...
10 and moreover, the rest of the gentlemen they imprisoned were bound with chains and locks and they appointed (guards) to prevent them from escaping.

(Adapted from Nicholas Sotherton, Commoyson in Norfolk, 1549)

Although this account was written from the viewpoint of the gentry it does give some indication of the atmosphere within the camp. Stories of gentry mistreatment soon circulated. One who tried to negotiate with the rebels took food and drink with him, but was still attacked and only just escaped with his life. As a result others soon fled, leaving the area in the hands of the commons.

Social tensions were also evident within Norwich. The inequality of wealth within the city, where 6 per cent of the population owned 60 per cent of the goods, made it vulnerable to class struggle. The decline of the local cloth industry only exacerbated the social and economic problems and may explain why the rebels were able to take the city so easily. Once in the city the behaviour of the insurgents reinforces the interpretation that the rebels were eager to show that they were more than a mere rabble. Private property was initially respected, but on the other hand after some of the citizens had let in Northampton's army, the rebels set fire to much of the city. But it was the houses of the rich and those who fled that received most of the damage.

This lack of respect towards their superiors was also shown on other occasions. The first instance was when Ket's army attacked Norwich. As Sotherton reports:

1   They were so shameless and so desperate that the poor vagabond boys, trouserless and bare arsed, came among the thickett of the arrows and gathered them up. When some of the arrows stuck fast in their legs and other parts they most shamefully turned up their bare
5   bottoms against those who did the shooting.

Secondly, when the rebels captured one of Northampton's mercenaries, they hung him over the city walls stripped naked as a sign of their contempt for his finery. Finally their treatment of the captured Lord Sheffield, who was brutally beaten to death, shows how some of the rebels showed their anger towards a hated ruling class. An examination of the management of the rebellion shows that, on the whole, the lower orders conducted their affairs well. This interpretation is supported by MacCulloch who argues that 'the frightening lesson of 1549 was that those outside the magisterial class could get on very well without them [gentry] until confronted with brute force.[5]

7 The Other Risings

> **KEY ISSUE** In what ways were the lesser risings a threat to the government?

Disturbances in 1549 were widespread. As the chart below shows, unrest affected at least 25 counties from the south to the north of England. It resulted in the loss of life and the destruction of property. Although most of the rebellions were easily put down by the local gentry some did require the use of government troops. However, it is essential to have an understanding of the lesser risings so that those in East Anglia and the West can be seen in a national context.

Month	Areas
March	Lincolnshire
May	Somerset, Wiltshire, Gloucestershire, Hampshire, Kent, Sussex, Essex, Staffordshire
June	Devon, Cornwall (Western Rising)
July	Northamptonshire, Bedfordshire, Oxfordshire, Buckinghamshire, Hertfordshire, Middlesex, Warwickshire, Suffolk, Yorkshire, Cambridgeshire, Norfolk (Ket's)
August	Leicestershire, Rutland.

Many of these disorders were the result of the long-term economic and religious developments outlined earlier. Although we have to be careful about being simplistic in our interpretation of the risings, it is clear that two causes stand out. The first was enclosure. Opposition to this was certainly evident in Lincolnshire, Hertfordshire, Cambridgeshire, Suffolk and Kent. Although the advantage of hindsight allows us to see that many of the disturbances were stopped before they had started or were no more than local protests, at the time they appeared to constitute a major challenge to the government. More importantly we must also remember that under slightly different circumstances they could have developed into major rebellions that rivalled those in East Anglia and the West. If the rebels had been able to find leaders of the calibre of Ket and co-ordinated their actions, the government would have faced a major crisis.

The second cause of the trouble appears to have been religion. This appears to be the case in at least Oxfordshire, Hampshire and Yorkshire. Contemporaries blamed these risings on catholics who were opposed to the religious innovations. Although we have to be careful about accepting these views at face value, there is certainly evidence that local clergy were hard at work encouraging the risings. In many instances the clergy even assumed the leadership. But single cause explanations are unlikely to reveal the whole truth and many of the rebellions were a combination of economic and religious grievances.

8 The Defeat of Rebellion

> **KEY ISSUE** Why were the Western Rebellion and Ket's rising able to develop into serious challenges?

Although 1549 witnessed a large number of risings only the Western and Ket's required the government to commit large military forces to defeat them. Why was it that these risings developed into large scale challenges? Most risings were usually dealt with at a local level by the resident nobilty or gentry, yet in both instances these groups were either absent or unable to act in face of the massive demonstrations. This gave the rebels the chance to increase their numbers and present an even greater challenge. As soon as they were able to either seize or beseige a major city the government had to take the threat seriously.

However, the government was not always aware of the seriousness of the situation. This was particularly true of the Western Rebellion. It was some time before the government knew that the rising had spread from Sampford Courtenay and had joined with the Cornish rebellion. At the same time the government were faced with many other uprisings that required action and also with the threat of an invasion from France. All of this gave the Western Rebellion and Ket's the chance to develop.

Given the other problems faced by Somerset, it is hardly surprising that the government had tried the traditional methods of appealing to the rebels to disperse and offering a pardon. Both of these had the advantage of not costing the government money or requiring the use of troops that Somerset needed for his campaigns in Scotland and to counter the possible invasion. Even after deciding that force was needed commanders found that they were diverted to deal with other troubles. This meant that it was a considerable time from the start of the risings to the arrival of a sufficiently large force to defeat the rebels.

9 The Significance of the Risings

KEY ISSUE How close was the monarchy to collapse in 1549?

The large number of risings suggests that there was a crisis in mid-Tudor England. The situation appears even more difficult when it is remembered that the government was weak: this was not the powerful regime of Henry VIII, but a newly established minority government which might not be able to count upon the support of the political nation. The policies they followed did not always have support and some questioned the legality of the religious changes they were implementing. The large number of risings stretched the government's resources to the limits and foreign wars and threats of invasion only added to their difficulties. Two of the risings had to be put down using full-scale military force. However, historians still disagree about the significance of the risings as these two extracts show:

1   The 1549 revolts were the closest thing Tudor England saw to a
     class war. No single cause was responsible: agrarian, fiscal, religious and
     social grievances fused. It was a hot summer and the crops failed; prices
     rose and the Protector compounded the problem by fixing maximum
5   prices at terrifyingly high metropolitan levels.
        Somerset mishandled the revolts. He vacillated in the spring of 1549
     not wishing to disrupt his Scottish campaign. He relied on pardons and
     proclamations and was criticised for ignoring the Council's advice. In July
     he ordered military reprisals without scruple and cancelled his Scottish
10   project, but the charge of procrastination levelled against him turned into
     an accusation of unwarranted leniency, even sympathy with the rebels.[6]

This view of Somerset's handling of the disturbances is in direct contrast to that of Michael Bush in his study of Somerset:

1   In quelling disorder, the government's policy towards the rebellions
     of 1549 was eminently successful. Most of the risings were dispersed as
     the government intended, with minimal effort and expense. This was
     true of both the spring risings and the summer ones. Plenty of evidence
5   continued to justify the government's initial policy of delaying direct
     military action, and the year demonstrated that the traditional offer of
     a royal pardon and promises of remedy was the most effective way to
     subdue peasant rebels. Furthermore, in the exceptional circumstances
     where the government applied the sword, it easily accomplished its
10   objective without heavy losses of capital and men.
        While sympathetic towards certain of the grievances which the
     rebels professed, his [Somerset's] attitude towards rebellion was one of
     conventional antipathy. His policy towards rebellion stemmed not from
     radical sentiments but from his urgent need to wage war, as well as to
15   demonstrate the efficacy of redressing social ills as a means of quelling
     disorder. When conciliation failed, he proceeded to use force.[7]

In order to reach a conclusion about the threat the risings presented it is necessary to ask – what were the aims of the rebels, did they seek to overthrow the regime, or were they trying to restore what they perceived to be the natural order and punish those who had overturned it? Whatever the answer, there were members of the ruling class who were not prepared to wait and find out. They acted quickly, removed Somerset and followed a policy of repression.

References

1 John Guy, *Tudor England*, p. 208.
2 E.A. Wrigley and R.S. Schofield, *The Population History of England 1541–1871: A Reconstruction* (2nd Edition, CUP, 1989), pp. 531–2, 568.
3 M.L. Bush, *The Government Policy of Protector Somerset* (Edward Arnold, 1975), p. 58.
4 Barrett L. Beer, *Rebellion and Riot: Popular Disorder in England during the Reign of Edward VI* (Kent State University Press, 1982) p. 55.
5 D. MacCulloch, *Ket's Rebellion in Context* (Past and Present 84, 1979), pp. 58–9, also reprinted in P. Slack (ed.) *Rebellion, Popular Protest and the Social Order in Early Modern England* (CUP, 1984).
6 John Guy, *Tudor England*, pp. 208–210.
7 M.L. Bush, *The Government Policy of Protector Somerset* (Edward Arnold, 1975) p. 97.

Summary Diagram
The 1549 Rebellions: A Comparison

WESTERN REBELLION		KET'S REBELLION
Conservative	← RELIGION →	Evangelical
Sheep Tax	← ECONOMIC →	Rents
Servants	← SOCIAL →	Society of Orders
Crispin & Moreman	← LOCAL GRIEVANCES →	Farming and Local Government
Treatment of Gentry	← CLASS CONFLICT →	Treatment of Gentry
Pole	← GOVERNMENT →	Local Officials
Attack gentry	← FORCE →	Burn Norwich
Exeter	← REGIONAL CAPITAL →	Norwich

Source-based questions on Chapter 4

There is one other type of source-based question that you are likely to encounter, that is the comparison between two documents.

1. The Western Rebellion
Read Articles 1, 2, 7, 8 and 9 of the Western Rebels' demands on page 53 and Article 8 of the Norfolk rebels on page 56.

a) Compare the view of the Western Rebels and Ket's rebels towards the role of the clergy. (*20 marks*)

When tackling this question it is again important that you do as the question requires and compare the documents. That does not mean that you write one paragraph on one source and another on the other source: if you do that you will be fortunate to score half marks. Instead you need to look for points of similarity and difference; these may be in their attitude to a particular issue or in why they were written. In this example, both sources want the clergy to preach, but Ket's rebels place a much greater emphasis on this ability and want those who are unable to fulfil this requirement to be removed. You should also draw attention to the fact that Ket's rebellion was more forward looking in its religious demands, suggesting that parishioners should be able to choose their own priests, whilst the Western rebels took a more conservative view of the role of the priest. You would need to explain this and show how they wanted a return to the sacred nature of the priesthood.

2. Sotherton's views
Read the two descriptions by Nicholas Sotherton of the behaviour of the rebels on page 59.

a) Explain the reference on page 59 to 'the tree of Reformation'. (*10 marks*)
b) How reliable is Sotherton's account of the behaviour of the rebels? (*20 marks*)
c) 'Ket's rebellion was no more than a protest or demonstration.' How far do the sources and your own knowledge support this view? (*60 marks*)

   Sometimes the examination boards also require you to contrast the views of historians. This can be tackled in the same way as the comparison of two sources.

3. Historians' views
Read the descriptions of the 1549 risings by John Guy and Michael Bush on pages 62–3.
   Compare the two views of Somerset's handling of the risings. (*20 marks*)

5 Mary Tudor and the Struggle for the Throne

POINTS TO CONSIDER

This chapter focuses on the two major challenges to Mary's right to the throne. As you read the chapter you will need to consider the role religion played in both attempts to alter the succession. You will need to ask why Mary was able to establish herself on the throne and maintain her position in the face of two serious challenges. Throughout your reading you should be looking to build up a list of reasons for the failure of the rebellions, whilst deciding which presented the greatest threat.

KEY DATES

1553	May	Guildford Dudley, Northumberland's son, marries Lady Jane Grey
	June	The Devise for the Succession alters the Succession
	July 6	Death of Edward VI, Lady Jane Grey proclaimed Queen, Mary Tudor proclaims herself Queen
	July 6–19	Reign of Lady Jane Grey
	July 14	Duke of Northumberland reaches East Anglia to arrest Mary
	July 19	Mary Tudor officially proclaimed Queen
	Aug	Duke of Northumberland executed
	Oct–Nov	Parliament repeals many Edwardian religious laws
	Dec	Marriage Treaty between Mary and Philip presented to Council
1554	Jan	Marriage Treaty ratified
		Wyatt's Rebellion
	Jan 25	Wyatt raises his standard at Maidstone
	Feb	Wyatt enters London
	Feb 9	Elizabeth arrested for supposed involvement in Wyatt's rebellion
	Feb	Execution of Lady Jane Grey
	July	Marriage of Mary and Philip
	Nov	Pole arrives in England as Papal Legate
	Dec	Heresy Laws reintroduced
1555	Jan	Restoration of Papal Supremacy
	Feb	Heresy persecutions start
		Poor harvest
1556		Poor harvest
1557		Stafford Conspiracy
1558		Loss of Calais
		Death of Mary

1 Lady Jane Grey and the Succession

> **KEY ISSUES** Who was behind the plan to alter the succession?
> Why was Mary able to seize the throne and defeat Lady Jane
> Grey?

a) The Death of Edward VI

As the health of the king, Edward VI, deteriorated in the spring of
1553, a scheme was devised to alter the succession. The plan was to
place Lady Jane Grey, Henry VIII's great niece and the granddaugh-
ter of his sister Mary (see family tree on page 67) on the throne of
England, so excluding both Mary and Elizabeth. The origins of this
plan are still a matter of great debate among historians. Was it the
brainchild of a devoutly protestant king who wanted to prevent his
catholic half-sister inheriting; or did it originate with the power-
hungry Northumberland, who saw it as a way of maintaining his
power?

In order to understand which of these interpretations is more
likely, it is essential to have a clear grasp of the timing of the actual
events. According to the Succession Act of 1544, the crown was to pass
to Mary and then Elizabeth if Edward died childless. In his will, Henry
had then named as next in line the descendants of his younger sister,
Mary – Lady Frances Grey and her daughters – rather than his elder
sister. This was the situation until the spring of 1553 when Edward
signed 'the Devise' for the succession. This left the throne to the male
heirs of Lady Frances Grey and her daughters whilst excluding Mary
and Elizabeth. A few weeks before this, Guildford Dudley,
Northumberland's son, had married Lady Jane Grey. By the end of
May 1553 doctors reported that Edward's health was declining fast
and that he had, at best, two months to live. This threw the initial
devise into chaos. There were no male heirs of the Grey family and no
possibility that any could be born before Edward died. It was therefore in early June that the Devise was changed to make Lady Jane the
heir. Articles were drawn up and Councillors and other notable
people were forced to sign them so that they committed themselves
to the scheme.

Only with this outline firmly understood is it possible to answer the
question: Who was behind the scheme?

There is little doubt that Northumberland had a great deal to gain
from it. His son would be married to the queen and his political
future would be secure. It was the only way for him to keep power
because, once Mary became queen, his religious beliefs would dis-
qualify him from office. However, a careful examination of the
chronology shows that it is not that simple. When Guildford married
Jane she was not heir to the throne; Northumberland was simply

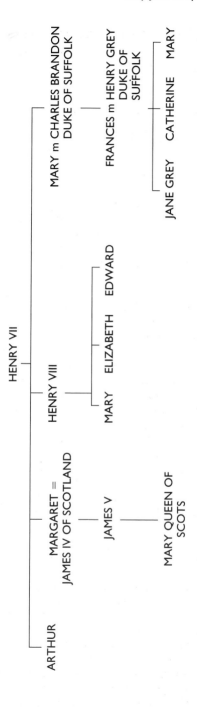

Family Tree and the Lady Jane Grey Affair

being a typical Tudor statesman and arranging a good marriage for his son. When the initial devise was drawn up the health of the king was such that it was expected that he would live for a long time. It was only when the devise was altered, because it was clear that Edward was dying, that Northumberland was suddenly raised in importance to be the father-in-law of the likely queen. If it was not the work of Northumberland, whose was it?

There are considerations that suggest the scheme was the work of Edward. Studies of his religious beliefs have suggested that he was a devout protestant, who was worried by the prospect of a catholic succession under his half-sister, Mary. More importantly, the inept handling of the whole plot suggests it was the work of an inexperienced mind. There is little doubt, given Northumberland's military skills, that if had he been involved in the planning he would have ensured that he had adequate forces available. Instead he dismissed his professional force in 1552. Secondly, he would have ensured that Mary was safely in custody and thus unable to rally forces. It is also likely that, with his political skills, he would have launched a careful propaganda campaign to prepare the nation for a change in the succession. There was a great deal of material available for such a campaign: he could have stressed Mary's catholicism, her illegitimacy and her likely dependence upon the Habsburgs. Therefore, despite a good motive, it is likely that the scheme originated with Edward. Certainly the devise was in his hand and, as recent work has shown, whilst he lived his word was law.

b) Did the plot stand a chance?

There are certainly reasons to suggest that it did. New research has shown that Northumberland had done a good job as Lord President following the removal of Somerset in October 1549.[1] He had brought the country stability and improved the financial situation. Many would have probably been willing to see this continue, even if it meant ignoring the lawful succession. However, the issue of the succession was not completely clear, and this could have helped Northumberland. The Succession Acts of 1534 and 1536 making Mary and Elizabeth illegitimate had not been repealed. A skilful politician such as Northumberland might be able to take advantage of this. He could also benefit from the fact that Tudor rule was not popular and that the prospect of another weak and female ruler would not appeal to those whose major concern was law and order and an avoidance of a return to the near anarchy of 1549. It was also obvious that if Mary came to the throne England would be taken back into the catholic fold. If the nation was protestant they would probably prefer the rule of Northumberland to continue. Meanwhile, on a more pragmatic level, those who had gained land from the Dissolution feared that Mary would seek to return it to the catholic church.

However, the fatal mistake had been made. Northumberland had failed to arrest Mary. Instead she had been allowed to escape from London and reach her supporters in East Anglia. This meant that if Northumberland were to seize the throne Mary would have to be captured, unless she surrendered without a struggle. This did not happen. Instead, Mary went to her own manor at Kenninghall, where many soon rallied to her cause. Why did so many support her? There is much debate about this, but two issues seem to have been important. The first was legitimacy. Despite the Succession Act, Henry's will had named Mary as queen and the Devise was an illegal attempt to subvert the 1544 Act. The question of legitimacy was very important for the landed class. If they supported an illegal claimant then all laws could be brought into question, and that could easily threaten their own land tenure. It was in their interests to support the rightful ruler, unless they wanted to encourage anarchy and a challenge to a system that had brought them great benefits. It is therefore hardly surprising that she was soon joined by many important national figures, as well as local gentry. Just as importantly, religious belief was not significant, for protestant gentry as well as catholic rallied to the cause, suggesting that legitimacy was the crucial factor. This fact was reinforced by Mary's own actions. She behaved as a monarch and proclaimed herself queen. She sent letters to the Privy Council and towns informing them of her succession. This made it clear that those who opposed her were opposing the rightful ruler, with all the implications that would bring once her position became secure. These actions forced people to make a choice between her and Jane.

However, it can be argued that religion was an important factor.[2] The politically aware knew that if Mary succeeded then a catholic restoration would take place. The protestant reformation had failed to win the hearts of the majority of the people, who were still catholic.[3] They welcomed the prospect of a catholic monarch, particularly as it was not certain that she would restore papal authority, or return monastic lands to the church. Certainly it was not apparent that she would act intolerantly.

Northumberland's great advantage had been his command of London, but even that was soon lost. With Mary rallying troops in East Anglia, he left the capital to go and meet her. From the moment of his departure his position deteriorated. Commentators noted that, as he left, 'no one says God speed'. His departure also gave the Privy councillors, who had been forced to agree to the change, the opportunity to reveal their true feelings. They soon declared themselves for Mary. Northumberland did not gain the support he needed as he made his way towards Mary. Whether this was due to his reputation for harsh rule, or because many in the area remembered his treatment of Ket's rebels (see page 56), is not clear, but what is certain is that many commoners now flocked to Mary. Northumberland was forced to withdraw and in the end proclaim Mary queen. Mary had staged the only successful English revolt of the entire century.[4] She had Northumberland, Lady Jane Grey and Guildford Dudley arrested and executed. Yet within a year she was to face another serious challenge to her rule and it would be led by Wyatt, a man who had rallied to Mary in 1553. What caused him to challenge the lawful monarch?

2 Wyatt's Rebellion

> **KEY ISSUES** What role did the Spanish marriage and religion play in Wyatt's rebellion? Why was the rising so limited? Did the rebellion stand a chance? Did it achieve anything?

a) The background

The immediate background to the rising was Mary's decision to marry Philip of Spain. However, whether this was the cause or simply the occasion of the rising is still a matter of debate. Mary was determined to marry for a variety of reasons. She believed that she needed a husband to help guide her through a male dominated world. More significantly, she wanted an heir as she was very concerned about the future of the dynasty, believing that her half-sister, Elizabeth, would not preserve the catholic faith. This mattered to Mary as she was the daughter of Catherine of Aragon and thus saw herself as a symbol of catholicism. Her religion had sustained her through the dark days of her father's rule and this, and her mother's background, meant that she felt an attachment to Spain. Moreover, her choice of potential husbands at home was severely limited. The only possible choice was Courtenay, but he was considered unsuitable, having been brought up in prison and lacking the necessary social graces. This meant that a foreign match was the most likely outcome. Although many princes were ready to wed the English queen, Philip offered much that appealed to Mary. He represented all that she trusted, being catholic and Spanish. The match was also encouraged by Philip's father, Charles V, who saw England as a potential counter to the French. It would make it that much easier for the Spanish to reach the Netherlands via the Channel.

However, no sooner were there rumours of marriage than opposition began to surface. The traditional suspicion and hatred of foreigners was aroused as many feared, irrationally, that it would lead to a foreign takeover. There were soon stories circulating that positions at court would go to foreigners and that England would be little more than a Spanish outpost as Mary was dominated by her husband. Even Mary's council and parliament voiced disapproval and, once news of the marriage became public, a proclamation had to be issued against 'Unlawful and rebellious assemblies'. This was soon followed by rumours of plots to remove Mary and replace her with Elizabeth. As the plans for the marriage became more serious, so rumours of a rebellion began to grow. The aim was to engineer a protestant succession, with Elizabeth married to Courtenay. By December these rumours had become an actual plot.

b) The Events

The plot involved four simultaneous rebellions in Kent, Devon, Leicestershire and on the Welsh borders. These risings were scheduled for March 1554. The plotters had secured foreign assistance in the form of aid from the French, who would provide naval help in securing ports in the south west of the country. However, by mid January the court was aware of the plotting through the Imperial Ambassador. An examination of Courtenay soon led to most of the story being revealed. Therefore, in order to retain the initiative, the conspirators decided to act at once. Unfortunately for them the timing was poor as winter was not a good time to persuade potential supporters to leave their homes. The four-pronged rising failed to get off the ground in Devon, Leicestershire or on the Welsh borders. In Devon they were probably still mindful of events in 1549 (see pages 52–5) whereas in both Leicestershire and Wales there was little support for the scheme and the leaders were soon arrested. The leadership of the rebellion had been caught out by the speed of events and, as a result, it was only in Kent, under the leadership of Wyatt, that anything occurred; and even he was unprepared for the early action that had been forced on them.

However, despite being forced to act quickly Wyatt was able to assemble a force of between 2,500 and 3,000 men. The Wyatt family had served the Tudor dynasty loyally and Thomas Wyatt was one of the leading Kent landowners. It was his standing within local society that enabled him to raise men quickly. However, he was unable to attract support from the nobility and had to rely for leadership on the social groups below the highest ranks. The lack of nationally known men among the leadership meant that, as they moved towards London, they were unable to attract others to join their cause and turn the rising into a large-scale revolt.

However, although the size of the force was small in comparison with the 30,000 of the Pilgrimage of Grace, it was a major concern for the government. Kent was close to London, the seat of power, and there was strong anti-Spanish feeling that could be tapped by the rebels. On January 25th 1553 Wyatt raised his standard at Maidstone and within two days had established his headquarters at Rochester. He was soon joined by further forces from other areas of the county, rallied by the anti-Spanish propaganda issuing from Wyatt's camp.

> Beware, the Spaniards have already arrived at Dover, at one count they number a hundred, they are moving on to London, in companies of ten, four and six, with harness, arquebuses, and helmets, with torches, the first company have already reached Rochester.[5]

Wyatt had shown how vulnerable the regime was. His clever propaganda, appealing to nationalism and xenophobia, had made it difficult for loyalists in Kent to rally forces against him.

Mary acted before the force grew any stronger and her response was to send troops under the aged Duke of Norfolk to meet the rebels. Unfortunately for her, this was a disaster. Many of the royal soldiers deserted to Wyatt with the cry 'We are all Englishmen'. This could have done little for either her, or the city of London's, confidence. Meanwhile, Wyatt's force had grown to some 3,000 and London appeared to be at his mercy. If he had moved quickly others would have joined him, but his delay was to prove fatal.

Over the next few days the situation changed dramatically. As at the start of her reign, adversity seemed to bring renewed strength and determination from the Queen. She was soon rallying the city with flattering words and a personal appeal which proclaimed Wyatt a traitor. Her refusal to leave the capital further strengthened the resolve of many. Meanwhile Wyatt had made his big mistake. He hesitated and, instead of marching straight for London, he delayed and went to Cooling Castle to seize Lord Cobham. This delay gave London a chance to prepare and London Bridge was fortified. Upon arrival the rebels again waited, uncertain as to their next action. The delays were sapping morale and Wyatt's force were hungry and weary. It was not until February 6 that they finally crossed the River Thames at Kingston and it was another day before they reached Knightsbridge. The main body of the rebel force was attacked, but Wyatt was able to proceed to Charing Cross where government forces fled at the first shot. Confusion and chaos followed and there were soon rumors of royal defeat as the rebels approached Ludgate. The mood of the crowd suggested that the result was still in the balance as locals drew back to allow Wyatt and his men to pass. However, Ludgate remained closed and the rebellion was defeated. Many who had allowed him to pass just moments earlier attacked as he retreated. Wyatt then decided to surrender. Despite Mary's astute handling of the situation it had been a close-run thing and it could quite easily have had a different outcome. Many of the queen's forces had put up only limited resistance and some troops had run once the first shots were fired. Finally, on February 9, Princess Elizabeth was arrested for supposed involvement in the plot.

c) What were the causes of the rising?

Historians have tended to be divided in their interpretation of the causes of the rising between those who see religion as the prime cause

Mary Tudor.

and those who see the Spanish marriage as the major reason for the rising. The only contemporary account available was written by John Proctor in 1554. However, his version of events was written from a government perspective and therefore must be treated with a certain amount of caution. Proctor was writing for a purpose and both he and the government wanted to show that the rising was caused by the catholic restoration and not the Spanish marriage. This would then allow the government to portray protestants as traitors and punish them accordingly. On the other hand, David Loades, writing more recently, has argued that 'the real reasons which lay behind the conspiracy were secular and political'.[6] Where does the truth lie? One of our problems in trying to answer this question is that religion was such a divisive issue in England that both Wyatt and Mary wanted to play down its importance. This means that contemporary sources tend to dismiss the issue. Wyatt himself was certainly well aware that claiming to rise for religion would limit the support he could draw on, as those who were catholic would not support him. Meanwhile opposition to the Spanish marriage could draw support from both sides of the religious divide.

However, although Proctor's purpose was to justify the regime's religious policies, there is a great deal to support his interpretation. According to Fletcher, the regional leaders of the supposed four-pronged attack all had at least some sympathies with protestantism; Carew had promoted it in the west country, Croft had introduced a protestant liturgy in Ireland and the Duke of Suffolk had been a patron of protestant clergy.[7] The only problem area was Wyatt himself, for he repudiated religion as a motive in the rising. An examination by Thorp has also revealed that the leading rebels had protestant leanings: of the 14 lay leaders, eight were definite protestants and three probable. Moreover, the only area where the conspiracy actually turned into revolt was Kent and that was a religiously radical area. Wyatt drew a large amount of his support from the area around Maidstone. This was a stronghold of protestantism and would provide the Marian regime with a large number of martyrs. Even the actions of the rebels suggest that religion might have played some role in the rising. Wyatt had received advice from Ponet, the recently deprived protestant Bishop of Winchester. On the other hand, no single prominent figure in the plot was catholic. Just as importantly, the only real evidence of violence once the rebels reached London was an attack on the property of Stephen Gardiner, the man who had replaced Ponet as Bishop of Winchester.

Despite this evidence it is difficult to reach a firm conclusion about the role religion played. Although the area of the revolt had strong protestant sympathies and many of those involved were protestant, this does not mean that the rebels rose for religious reasons. It is very difficult for the historian to provide evidence of a link, and perhaps the best that we can suggest is that religion was one reason among many – that for some it may well have been the most important, but that for others there were other more important concerns. They may have risen because they were more concerned by the marriage. This is certainly the view taken by most modern writers.

Wyatt himself declared publicly that he was only motivated by the issue of the marriage. However, as we have suggested, there were good propaganda reasons for such a statement and we should be careful in accepting it at face value. In such a religiously divided nation an appeal to patriotism would have a stronger appeal and might bring the conspirators much greater support. How many loyal Englishmen would be able to resist Wyatt's passionate appeal:

> Because you are our friends and because you are Englishmen you will
> join with us, as we will with you until we die, in this cause protesting

unto you before God ... We seek no harm to the Queen, but better counsel and councillors.

But this is propaganda and needs to treated with caution. Its purpose was to swell the numbers in the rising. The rebels knew that, by playing on the possible and potential damage that the marriage could bring to England, they could play on fears without the need for real evidence, for the fear of the unknown was more frightening for many than reality. They exploited and exaggerated the fears of what Philip might do once he was secure in England. It was easy to argue that he would dominate political life, government and court. Those who had been accustomed to receive rewards could soon find themselves pushed out as Spaniards got all the top jobs and access to patronage. Although this might not appeal to the masses it was bound to strike a chord in the upper echelons of society. Rumours that England would become little more than a satellite of the Habsburg Empire worried many (just as today the potential or perceived loss of national independence is a sure way to win support). It was argued that Philip would drag England into interminable European conflicts that did not concern her and would be a drain on resources as taxes would have to rise to support the conflicts. The fear for the future was further exploited by concern about the succession. What would happen if a child were to be born? What if Mary was to die in childbirth? The marriage treaty limited the powers of Philip, as only Englishmen were to fill offices, the nation's laws and customs were to be preserved and his rights were to die with Mary's death. However, there were fears that he would not keep his word. How could the treaty be enforced? Finally, what would happen to English liberties? The popular imagination had started to associate Spanish rule with harshness and it was not difficult for the rebels to argue that England could expect similar treatment. After all, had Ghent not just risen against the Habsburgs?

There was enough evidence to give these ideas credence and the audience in England was more than ready to listen. There was certainly anti Spanish feeling, shown clearly by the pelting of Philip's envoys with snowballs; and Wyatt and his followers were skilled in exploiting it. This hostility went beyond the confines of the area of the rebellion. As one Norwich carpenter commented on the prospects of the marriage, 'We will lie in pig sties in caves and the Spaniards will have our houses and we will live like slaves'. Hardly a rational response, or likely to be the outcome; but it reveals how deep the anti-Spanish feeling was and why Wyatt was astute in claiming it to be the reason for the rising. But for this very reason we must be careful not to see the revolt simply as a response to the marriage. It is likely that the motives were more complex.

It is possible to see other factors as important in encouraging the rising. It may not have been a coincidence that the only area where the rising actually got going had just experienced an economic slump. The cloth trade in Kent had suffered in the recent past and there had been rising unemployment in the area since 1551. Moreover, many of those who took part came from the Cranbrook area of the Weald, an area that had suffered particularly from this crisis. However, it is difficult to reach a conclusive answer as the list of rebels that we possess reveals occupations covering over 30 trades, and this makes it very difficult to be certain there was an economic pattern.

The other possible cause that has been identified, which would have been particularly important for those of a higher social status, is factional struggle. Mary's arrival on the throne had seen a shake-up in office holding and many had lost positions of influence in the local community. It is possible to see, in the leadership, prominent former members of the Edwardian regime who had struggled to keep Lady Jane Grey on the throne. With her defeat they had lost office and now saw this rebellion as their only hope of restoring their political fortune. The supposed arrival of a large number of Spaniards would further dent their hopes of returning to power. Although a desperate measure, rebellion was the only way to engage in the debate about royal policy and show opposition. It would not be until later, in Elizabeth's reign, that parliament would become the battleground in such struggles.

As we have seen, historians are divided as to the emphasis they place upon religious or political motives. Was Wyatt's rebellion a religious protest that should be placed in the same category as the Western Rebellion, or should we be looking back to the days of Perkin Warbeck and Henry VII and see it as an attempt to remove a reigning monarch? The answer, as with most of the Tudor rebellions, is likely to be a combination of many factors. For some religion would have been the driving force, whilst for others political considerations would have been the dominant factor. Each individual involved would have his reasons for rising and it is impossible for historians to discover the motives of the rank and file who made up the bulk of Wyatt's force. This may not be a satisfactory answer, but as historians we have to acknowledge that there will always be gaps in our understanding and that, at times, the best we can do is to offer suggestions, rather than pronounce definite answers.

d) Why did the Rebellion fail?

There are many reasons for its failure. Wyatt undoubtedly had his chances, but he made mistakes. In at least two instances he delayed, instead of moving quickly to London and forcing Mary to either abandon the marriage or be replaced by Elizabeth. This gave Mary vital time to prepare.

After the initial mistake of sending Norfolk to confront him, Mary handled the situation in a very skilful manner. Instead of moving from London and confronting the rebels, leaving London open to attack, she waited and forced them to try to take the city. Meanwhile the time was used to fortify the capital. For a second time she revealed her skill in a crisis. She ignored the advice of her advisors and remained in London. Her speech to the citizens also helped to inspire and rally them to her cause:

> Certainly if a prince and governor may as naturally and earnestly love her subjects as a mother loves her child, then assure yourselves that I, being your lady and mistress, do as earnestly and tenderly love and favour you.

Like her father Mary possessed the Tudor skill of flattery, but she was also able to play on the fear of destruction, should the rebels enter the city, and remind them of Cade's rising in 1450 (see page 2). Her persuasive skills brought their reward when Ludgate remained closed. Her political skills were also evident when she offered Wyatt a committee to discuss the rebels' grievances, and a pardon for those who went home. This delayed Wyatt further as the offer was considered and gave Mary more time to prepare. The offer of a pardon was also designed to divide the rebel force.

However, the reason for their defeat may actually be due to a deep-seated change in society's outlook towards rebellion. After the disorder and virtual anarchy of 1549 many did not want further chaos. The rebellion challenged the monarch's right to rule and even if Wyatt had been careful to conceal his goal of deposing the monarch, there was little doubt that it would be his only option once Mary had failed to agree to his demands. Most were not prepared to see another succession crisis so soon after the Lady Jane Grey affair. It was, after all, hardly 12 months since they had rallied to Mary's defence as the legitimate ruler; they were not going to abandon her now. Mary had not yet adopted the religious policies that would alienate many: the fires of Smithfield were still in the future, the legend of 'Bloody Mary' had not been made. Therefore loyalty to the legitimate ruler and a desire to avoid civil strife encouraged many to at least remain neutral and await the outcome. However, if this is true it was events in London that determined the outcome. If the citizens and city government had not rallied to Mary, Wyatt would have achieved his goal. This would suggest that the Marian regime had been seriously challenged.

e) What can be learned about the Marian regime from the rebellion?

During the rising many had remained neutral, waiting to see how events would unfold. The loss of support for Mary at Rochester had shown how weak the regime was. This, and the impact of Wyatt's message, encouraged many to play the waiting game. As Penry Williams argues, 'A crucial episode in Tudor history was thus determined with most of the political nation standing aside and even the active participants behaving equivocally and hesitantly'.[8] Although the rising lacked prominent national figures, it had come close to success. Why? There are two very clear reasons. The Spanish marriage was unpopular with many, who were therefore unwilling to rally to the defence of the crown. Secondly, unlike most other large-scale Tudor risings, this one had taken place close to London. It made it much easier for the rebels to strike at the very heart of the regime very quickly and before the forces started to desert. The defence of the capital depended upon controlling the surrounding area, but events at Rochester had shown that, at least temporarily, Mary had lost the support of the south east, leaving her capital open to attack and her future as queen uncertain.

The weakness of the regime is also shown by the events that followed the rebellion. After the Pilgrimage of Grace Henry had made an example of the rebels with summary executions. Mary, on the other hand, did not implement a punitive campaign. This was probably because she was aware that there was a great deal of latent sympathy for the rebels and that any attempt to exact revenge would lead to further unrest. Despite her victory she was aware that her position was vulnerable. She had fewer than 100 rebels executed and, unlike her predecessors, did not have the bodies dispatched to various parts of the kingdom in order to overawe the people. It can even be argued that the only reason Mary did not have either Elizabeth or Courtenay executed for their supposed involvement in the plot was that she was astute enough to realise that it could be the signal for further unrest and lose the weak regime further support.

However, even in defeat it can be argued that the rebellion did have an impact. By turning their attention to parliament the gentry were able to ensure that there were changes to royal policy. In the short term their greatest achievement was in preventing the coronation of Philip. This was an affront to his dignity and may well have influenced his opinion of England, encouraging him to spend as little time as possible in the country, thus helping to ensure that there was no catholic succession! It also ensured that Mary's plan to disinherit Elizabeth by statute did not happen, further ensuring a protestant succession. Lastly, Mary was realistic enough to abandon any plans she might have had to try to restore former monastic lands to the church. It is therefore possible to suggest that even if Wyatt failed to remove Mary and replace her with Elizabeth in the short term, he did ultimately, perhaps indirectly, achieve his goal of ensuring a protestant nation. In achieving success in influencing policy through parliament the gentry may also have seen that this was the best way forward in the future, rather than risking life and limb in rebellion.

3 Conclusion

> **KEY ISSUE** Was the Lady Jane Grey affair or Wyatt's rebellion the greater threat to the Tudor monarchy?

Both rebellions came close to overthrowing the monarchy. Northumberland had Jane crowned, whilst Wyatt got to the city gates. There is little doubt that if Northumberland had been involved in the plot at an earlier stage he would have prevented Mary's departure to East Anglia. If this had happened he would have stood a real chance as he controlled the city, the Tower and the Mint. He would not have needed to leave London, a vital factor as was shown by Mary during Wyatt's revolt. Northumberland was a leading peer of the realm and thus able to coerce many into supporting the scheme, whereas Wyatt was only a member of the gentry class and unable to win over influential support. Perhaps if all four prongs of the attack had occurred the threat would have been serious.

Yet, despite his many weaknesses Wyatt came very close to success. In 1553 Mary had not alienated important sections of the nation, but by the time of the marriage she had done enough to cause many to wait and see, giving Wyatt a chance. A quick attack on London might have overcome all his difficulties. Instead, when success seemed to beckon, he hesitated and delayed, giving Mary vital time. One thing does seem clear: when her position was threatened Mary behaved like a queen, acting decisively, either sending out letters or refusing to leave her capital. In both instances a good case can be made for seeing the queen as the major cause of the defeat of rebellion. In the end, both failed because the country did not want the disorder that a disputed succession would bring. As the Wars of the Roses had shown, things had to be very bad before those with political power were prepared to risk their land and possessions in an attempt to overthrow the legitimate monarch.

References

1 Dale Hoak, 'Rehabilitating the Duke of Northumberland', in *Mid Tudor polity 1540–1560*, eds. Loach and Titler (Macmillan, 1980), pp. 29–51.
2 Jennifer Loach, *Edward VI* (Yale, 1999) is a new work that argues that religion was the deciding factor, see page 164.
3 Christopher Haigh, *English Reformations* (OUP, 1993), argues that England was still largely catholic on Mary's accession, see p. 205.
4 Robert Titler, *The Reign of Mary Tudor* (Longman, 1987), p. 12.
5 John Proctor, *The Historie of Wyate's Rebellion* (1554).
6 David Loades, *Two Tudor Conspiracies* (CUP, 1965), p. 88.
7 Anthony Fletcher and Diarmaid MacCulloch, *Tudor Rebellions* (Longman, 1997), p. 92.
8 Penry Williams, *The Later Tudors* (OUP, 1995), p. 96.

Summary Diagram
Mary Tudor and the Struggle for the Throne: Cause and Failure

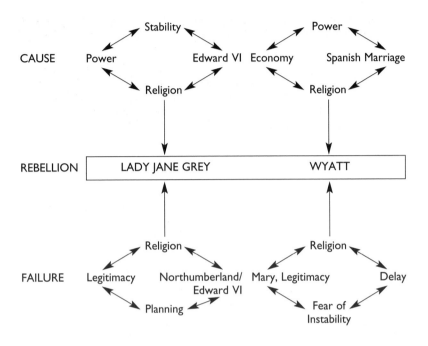

Essay Questions on Chapter 5

1. Estimate the relative significance in the attempt to replace Mary Tudor with Lady Jane Grey of Edward VI, the Duke of Northumberland and Lady Jane Grey herself.
2. Did Wyatt's rebellion and the outcome demonstrate the strength or weakness of the government of Mary?
3. How far was Wyatt's rebellion from achieving its goals?
4. Which was the greater threat to Mary, the Lady Jane Grey affair or Wyatt's rebellion and why?

6 Elizabeth I and the Defeat of Rebellion

POINTS TO CONSIDER

This chapter deals with the three major rebellions that faced Elizabeth: the rising of the Northern Earls, Oxfordshire and Essex. You should be aware of the causes of each rebellion and the light they shed upon the problems faced by Elizabeth. However, these rebellions help to show reasons for the decline in rebellion. You should consider why Elizabeth was able to rule for so long with little serious challenge to her position.

KEY DATES

1558	November	Elizabeth succeeds to the throne
1559	January	Elizabeth displays her disapproval at the elevation of the host during communion
	May	Acts of Supremacy and Uniformity
	July	Royal Injunctions on religious beliefs
		Mary Stuart arrives in England
		Plot to marry Norfolk to Mary Stuart
	October	Norfolk sent to the Tower
		Rebellion of the Northern Earls
	December	Northern Rebellion collapses
1570	February	Northern Earls Rebellion finally defeated in Cumberland
		Papal Bull excommunicates Elizabeth
		Duke of Norfolk executed for treason
1596		Oxfordshire Rising
1600	June	Essex condemned to lose all his offices and imprisoned
	August	Essex released from prison
1601	January	Essex Rebellion
	February	Essex executed

1 The Elizabethan Succession

> **KEY ISSUE** Why was there no opposition to Elizabeth's succession?

Many contemporaries were surprised that there was no large-scale rebellion when Elizabeth ascended the throne of England in 1558. Her father, Henry VIII, had declared Elizabeth illegitimate when she was only three years old and this stigma had not been entirely removed even when this decision was reversed in 1543. Then, on the orders of her half sister Mary, she had been sent to the Tower, via Traitor's Gate, and had been fortunate to escape with her life following Wyatt's rebellion in 1554. The experience of Mary's reign may also have served to reinforce the sixteenth-century belief that women did not have the capacity to rule and were unable to control men or keep order. Elizabeth herself was also at a disadvantage as she had never been taught the skills needed for ruling a country. The country was still largely catholic, despite the Marian persecution, and Elizabeth's well-known protestant sympathies would also have made her an unattractive prospect. Why then was there no rebellion?

There are many reasons why Elizabeth's accession was peaceful and why it was a further 11 years before she faced a major disturbance. Although Elizabeth had been bastardised, she was still the daughter of Henry VIII and the loyalty to the Tudor dynasty that we have already seen help Mary gain the throne in 1553 may have done the same for Elizabeth: after all, she was, like her half sister, a Tudor.

Many in England wanted stability, as the years since the death of Henry VIII had seen England lurch from one crisis to another. This was particularly true under Edward VI, when there was concern that there would be a return to the disorder that had been prevalent during the Wars of the Roses. The nation wanted strong and firm government so that such horrors could be avoided. They were therefore willing to give Elizabeth a chance: she was the legal claimant and, after the disasters of the last years of Mary, many actually welcomed her. Mary had alienated large numbers by her Spanish marriage and reliance upon Spanish advisors; the religious persecution had not been popular; and the disastrous war with France, culminating in the loss of Calais, had further damaged her reputation. Elizabeth was therefore able to count on a reservoir of goodwill.

Elizabeth also possessed many qualities that would help her. Although only 25 and never taught the skills needed to rule, she had developed many of the necessary qualities whilst surviving during Mary's reign. She was intelligent and charming, but also cunning. This was to prove crucial in the early days of her rule. Most importantly, she acted and behaved like a queen who expected obedience. As Feria, the Spanish ambassador, recorded: 'she seems to me incomparably more feared than her sister and gives her orders and has her way as absolutely as her father did'.

Her intelligence and political skills were clearly seen in her early actions. The coronation was performed quickly in order to make it clear that there was no doubt about her right to be queen. It was turned into a spectacle, designed to create an image of splendour and power. Pageants en route were used to stress her special role, to show that she was worthy of the throne and that she was protestant. The final message of the procession stressed that she was Deborah 'the judge and restorer of Israel', God's chosen deliverer from the horrors of Mary's reign. Furthermore the council she established helped to bring stability. Although she removed many Marian councillors she did have the sense to keep those who wielded enormous power: men such as the Earls of Arundel, Pembroke, Derby and Shrewsbury.

Elizabeth I.

Elizabeth showed that she was willing to give to any, including religious conservatives, the benefits of her patronage if they did not uphold the Roman supremacy. At the same time she moved quickly to arrest or disarm potential opponents. Bishop White of Winchester, who had used Mary's funeral to warn his audience of the dangers of heresy under Elizabeth, was arrested. The same held true at a local level. There was no great purge of local officers, as she did not wish to alienate them. In all her actions the same message is clear: she wanted to exclude as few of her subjects as possible from her favours.

The religious policies also helped to prevent disorder. She kept the likely direction of her religious settlement obscure. The Acts of Uniformity and Supremacy were carefully worded to give hope to all her subjects. The Supremacy Act did not make her Head of the church, allowing catholics the opportunity to accept her title as they believed that the Pope was the head of the church on earth. Catholics were not seriously persecuted; therefore they had little reason to revolt. Elizabeth was also fortunate that the catholic community was in a state of confusion. This is made clear in the recent work of Jones: 'The Catholics of England did not immediately revolt, remaining passive, confused by the lack of direction from their leaders, and lulled by the gentleness of their queen's settlement'.[1]

The situation for catholics was further complicated by the Pope. He did not encourage them to revolt, hoping that Elizabeth and England would remain members of the catholic fold. This allowed them to live with the regime. Meanwhile, Philip II was unwilling to become embroiled in English affairs or provide foreign help to potential rebels for many reasons. Firstly, he hoped that he would be able to secure Elizabeth's hand in marriage and therefore was unwilling to offend her. So long as Elizabeth did not refuse his offers he would not support internal dissent or papal interference. Secondly Philip had little to gain from supporting a catholic rebellion. The catholic claimant was Mary Queen of Scots, who was pro-French. Spain was therefore unwilling to act against Elizabeth, fearing that England would be taken over by a Franco-Scottish alliance. If this was to happen it would put the Channel into French hands and threaten Spanish control over the Netherlands. As a result, Spain supported Elizabeth and did not provide the help that a successful rebellion would need.

As we have indicated, although at first sight Elizabeth's position was weak, there were many reasons why she was able to survive relatively comfortably the opening years of her reign. However, it is the job of historians to decide the relative importance of the various factors that allowed her to maintain the throne. It is here that a comparison with Mary Tudor may help in reaching a decision. As a result, some historians would suggest that, as with Mary, it was not her religion but legitimacy and the Tudor name that was the greatest advantage she possessed. In addition to this, it must not be forgotten that she was fortunate with the foreign situation and skilled enough to be able to exploit both this and the weakness of her opponents at home.

2 The Northern Rebellion

KEY ISSUE What developments changed the situation for Elizabeth?

a) Background

Elizabeth had survived her early years and by the later 1560s must have felt reasonably secure. However, changes at home and overseas altered the political situation in England and caused the first and only major challenge to Elizabeth's rule. As with all Tudor rebellions, historians have different views about the causes. In many ways the Northern Rebellion of 1569 appears to be the most simple: it was surely a response to the changing religious situation in England and the arrival of a focus, Mary Queen of Scots, for the catholics. However, as with most events, it is not that simple.

To understand the Northern Rebellion it is essential to place it in the context of the changing domestic and international situation. On the surface everything appeared to be calm. Catholicism had been Elizabeth's greatest threat in 1558, yet by the 1560s this was no longer the case. Although there were still some clergy who followed catholic practices, it was gradually being confined to the households of landowners. It appeared as if catholicism might simply die out. Gradually many were turning to protestantism, or at least conforming, seeing the political advantages and prospect of rewards in such a move. The catholic threat from abroad was no greater, as neither the Pope nor Philip was willing to take a lead in trying to dethrone Elizabeth. The Pope hoped that it would be possible to maintain links with England. He wanted Elizabeth to send representatives to the Council of Trent that was meeting to spearhead reform in the Catholic Church. It was only in 1562 that he finally prohibited catholics from attending Anglican services. Philip, the European champion of catholicism, had his own problems and did not wish to become involved in foreign adventures. Moreover, a persistent suitor, he still held hopes of marrying Elizabeth and went as far as putting pressure on the Pope not to excommunicate her for fear of destroying his chances. In these circumstances it appeared that the Queen did not need to act, for her policies had not aroused displeasure and, unlike Mary Tudor, she had not made the mistake of creating martyrs.

Given the appearance of tranquillity, what changes took place and provided the background for the unrest? There were three events of crucial importance. Firstly, the Calvinist rebels in the Netherlands appeared to have been defeated by the Spanish in May 1567. As a result Spain was in a stronger position to intervene in English affairs, and this became more likely when Elizabeth's chief minister, William Cecil, impounded the Spanish bullion ships in December 1568. They had been bound for the Spanish army in the Netherlands, but had been chased by privateers and sought refuge in west-country ports, whereupon Elizabeth seized the bullion. This act prevented the army from being paid and ended the friendship that had existed between the countries since 1558-9. Cecil appeared to be taking England closer to a war with Spain and this caused consternation among many at court. Might the nobility, who disliked both his dominance and his policies, be prepared to use this action to encourage, or even support, rebellion? Mary Queen of Scots had fled to England in May 1568 and could provide the focus for a rising. She was, in the eyes of many catholics, the rightful ruler of England, and as Elizabeth was not married and refused to resolve the succession question, Mary was the likely heir.

Although catholicism was declining, Christopher Haigh's study of Tudor Lancashire shows that it was still strong in the North, where the protestant reformation had failed to take hold. Catholics were still appointed as JPs. Yet these were the very men whose job it was to impose the new religion and drive out the old! Even where Elizabeth could remove catholic priests, it was difficult to obtain trained and educated protestants to replace them. The Reformation in the north was a slow process and the trouble that the Pilgrimage of Grace caused Henry (see pages 41–2) shows how strong ties to the old religion were. Given this, it is perhaps hardly surprising that Mary Queen of Scots' arrival in the north of England provided the spark for rebellion.

b) The Events of 1569–1570

Parliament had tried to raise the succession question in 1566 but Elizabeth, as usual, had refused to discuss the matter. However, the arrival of Mary in England reopened the debate. At court an anti-Cecil faction devised a plan to marry Mary to the Duke of Norfolk, the greatest of the English nobles. They believed that this would force Elizabeth to name Mary as heir and would force Cecil out. The plotters were convinced that Cecil was taking England close to war with France and Spain, whereas the marriage would ensure peace. They also believed that once Mary had married she would turn protestant, although there is little evidence to support this. The scheme was supported by two northern earls, the Earl of Northumberland, who had been reconverted to catholicism in 1567, and the Earl of Westmorland, a devout catholic. The Earls, on the other hand, believed that the marriage would bring a catholic succession nearer and were willing to conspire in order to achieve their aim. Hence they had already been in touch with Rome and Spain for military help to further the marriage.

The proposed plan did not escape Elizabeth's ears for long. The Queen was quick to express her displeasure and vetoed the proposal. Upon discovering that the Queen did not approve of the marriage Norfolk begged for Elizabeth's mercy. He was lucky: a brief spell in the Tower was his punishment. At this point it is highly unlikely that there were any plans for a rebellion. Indeed Norfolk had told both Northumberland and Westmorland not to rebel. However, when Elizabeth summoned the two Earls to court, the situation changed. Instead of going to court, they returned north. Encouraged by their wives, they raised their followers in rebellion.

Having decided to rise, the Earls marched on Durham. On November 14th 1569 the cathedral was seized, the Protestant communion table was thrown out and the catholic mass was heard. The rebels now marched towards Bramham Moor, near York. Perhaps their intention was to head south to Tutbury and release Mary Queen of Scots, who was being held there. However, this was as far south as they went, for on November 24th they turned back north, perhaps fearing rumours of the size of the royal force being sent to meet them. Their plan to free Mary was abandoned.

They now proceeded to capture Barnard Castle and Hartlepool, the latter providing them with a port through which foreign help could arrive. But with no foreign help apparent and news of the royal force having reached the River Tees, the Earls disbanded their forces on December 16th. A rebellion that had begun in early November 1569 was over by Christmas. However, in January 1570 another rebellion started under the leadership of Lord Dacre. He raised some 3,000 troops before he was defeated in battle near Carlisle. After a cold winter on the run, many of the rebels fled across the border to Scotland, including the Earl of Northumberland. Elizabeth ordered the execution of some 700 rebels, but in the end only 450 met that fate. The Earl of Northumberland was returned to England by the Scots in 1572 and was executed.

3 The Causes of the Rebellion of the Northern Earls

KEY ISSUES What were the causes of the Rebellion? Why did it fail?

There is no simple explanation for the events of late 1569. However, historians have tended to concentrate on three major areas to explain the rising, with the emphasis varying from one writer to another. Earlier rebellions should also have taught us that when trying to determine the causes of revolt a close examination of the events also

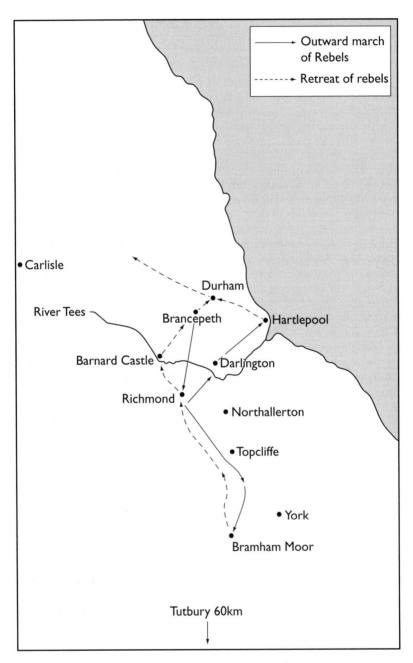

The Rising of the Northern Earls

helps us to understand the reasons behind the disturbances. Why, for example, was it the Earls of Northumberland and Westmorland who rose? Why did the rebels restore mass in Durham Cathedral?

a) Political factors

The two Earls had many reasons for leading the rising. Two reasons suggest themselves at this stage. Firstly, fear appears to be an important factor: they had already suffered a loss of status under the Elizabethan regime and now the failure of the marriage plan indicated that any hope of improvement in their position was finished. This interpretation is supported by the comment of a royal official: 'Sir I take this gathering is done more out of fear, than they want to carry out any evil act'. This view is further supported by the fact that they had no clear plan of campaign, suggesting that the rising was a sudden response to circumstances, namely fear if they did return to court. Therefore it may be possible to argue that the rising was a spontaneous reaction to the failure of the marriage plan. Secondly, the role of their wives in encouraging rebellion must not be discounted. The two Earls were both rather feeble and lacked energy, whereas the wives were dominant figures. Westmorland's wife was convinced that if they did not rise, then 'we and our country would be shamed for ever, and now in the end we should seek holes to creep into'.

The ancient nobility of the north had become increasingly alienated from court. They felt insecure following the attacks on their positions by Henry VIII, Edward and now Elizabeth. Jobs that had traditionally gone to local families were going to outsiders. Lawrence Stone described the revolt as 'the last episode in 500 years of protest by the Highland zone against the interference of London'.[2] The Earls represented those excluded and replaced. An examination of the rebels' proclamation issued at Darlington in November supports this interpretation: 'There are a variety of new nobles about the Queen's majesty ... who not only go about to overthrow and put down the ancient nobility of this realm, but have also misused the Queen's Majesty's own person'.[3] The Earls were desperate men and this was perhaps their last throw of the dice to restore their fortunes. Northumberland had been created Lieutenant General of the North by Mary in 1558. This had given him great prestige in the area. However, Elizabeth had not shown him such favour. She had not allowed him to play any role in the custody of Mary Queen of Scots and had also allowed his commission as Lieutenant to lapse. These moves were an affront to the Earl's dignity and a sign that he could expect no favours from Elizabeth. Instead the Queen had brought in her own followers. As a consequence Northumberland was declining in both wealth and status. Westmorland was no different. His poverty was so great that he had had to borrow money in order to remain solvent. Like Northumberland, he felt excluded; there was no hope of reward that would take him out of his penury.

Was there a regional crisis? It certainly appears as if those accustomed to royal favour and reward felt excluded and ignored. This view is supported by some of the most recent work on the rebellion. Revisionist historians have argued that it was more than a response to the Norfolk marriage and should be seen as a reaction to the longer process of the extension of crown power in the north. This culminated in the appointment of a protestant exile, James Pilkington, as Bishop of Durham. Elizabeth's cousin, Lord Hunsdon, was given control over important border areas and the Queen built up the power of Sir John Foster, one of Northumberland's rivals. Excluded, the Earls may well have felt that their choice was either to flee or to rebel.

b) Religious factors

The official view was that the rebellion was to resist the new religion, which would explain the resentment felt at the appointment of a protestant Bishop of Durham. Even in one of the more recent studies the writers identify a strong catholic influence in the people who launched the revolt.[4] However, does that prove that their motive was religious, or simply that those who were involved were catholic?

Those who argue that religion was the major cause of the rising stress the growing resentment at the influx of a new brand of militant protestants into the diocese of Durham, culminating in the appointment of Pilkington as Bishop. He gathered around him a group of senior protestant clergy who were aggressive in their promotion of change. They led a fierce assault on images within the local churches, they removed church furniture and led a drive to regain church lands that had been leased out. Perhaps it is hardly surprising that one of the first actions of the rebels should have been the seizure of Durham Cathedral. They entered the cathedral carrying a banner showing the Five Wounds of Christ, bringing back memories of the Pilgrimage of Grace. The rebels proceeded to destroy English Bibles, set up stone altars and holy water stoops and reinstate mass in Latin. The service was well attended, suggesting at least sympathy for the old religion. This view is supported by popular action elsewhere in the north: the protestant service book was destroyed in about 70 churches in Yorkshire and eight in Durham, whilst the mass was restored in at least six Yorkshire churches and a further eight in Durham. These actions were popular according to the Royal commander, Sir Ralph Sadler, because 'The ancient faith still lay like lees at the bottom of men's hearts and if the vessel was stirred a little came to the top'.

Royal officials were not the only ones who believed that religion was the driving force behind the rising and the rebel proclamation at Darlington also had a religious content. It accused the government of setting 'up and maintaining a new found religion and heresy, contrary to God's word'.[5] The Earl of Sussex also believed that religion was the cause, and although he did not leave York and might not

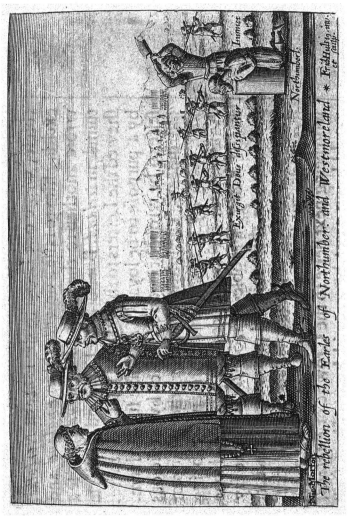

A picture from 'A Thankfull Remembrance of God's Mercie' published after Elizabeth's death. It shows the Earls of Westmorland and Northumberland ploting with a representative of the Church against Elizabeth. The background shows the defeat of the rebels and execution of Northumberland.

know the exact state of affairs, his view was supported by both the Vice President of the Council of the North and the commanders of the royal forces. The latter stated that 'all Cleveland, Allertonshire, Richmondshire, and the Bishopric completely support them, such is their devotion to the cause of religion'.

It appears as if two of the leading agitators behind the rebellion, Markenfeld and Norton, were motivated by religious fervor. They had just returned from trips abroad and were fired with the zeal of the Counter Reformation. This was the view reported to Cecil: 'the rebellion was one of the strangest matters that has been heard of and largely the work of Old Norton and Markenfeld'. Markenfeld was no stranger to revolt, having been involved in the Pilgrimage of Grace, and the similarity of the actions taken by the rebels and the symbols used does suggest at least some continuity between the two disturbances.

Religion appears to be the driving force for many. Catholicism had brought the rebellion most of its support. However, it would be wrong to see this is as the only reason. We will never discover the individual motives of each rebel and, although catholicism was still very strong in the north, we must not assume that because of this religion was the only, or even the major, cause. The Earl of Westmorland when asked to rise for religion was quick to reply: 'No ... those who quarrel for that reason in other countries, are accounted as rebels; and therefore I will never put a blot on my house, which has been for a long time preserved without staining'. However, once the rebellion had started the Earl claimed it *was* for religion. The historian must decide which of the Earl's comments is more reliable. Was he just using religion as a cloak for his political goal? Was religion the easiest way of ensuring widespread support for the cause?

In coming to a conclusion about the role of religion in the rising we must not dismiss it, but perhaps its importance is not as great as was once thought. A closer examination of religious belief in the north suggests that for the great majority catholicism was habitual and uninformed. It provided a set of rituals which gave meaning to people's daily lives, helping them to understand the seasons of the year, birth, death and marriage. Would this provide a sufficient motive for the rising? A comparison with the Pilgrimage of Grace may provide us with an even clearer understanding. In 1536, religion may have played a crucial role as the pilgrims feared Henry's changes. The Reformation had only just started and the rebels did not know what was going to happen. However, in 1569, there was no longer a fear of the unknown. The Reformation had not brought about major changes in their lives and although they may have disliked protestantism, it had not destroyed their way of life. Rebellion in the name of religion might actually force Elizabeth to take severe action against catholics.

c) The role of Bastard Feudalism

The development of bastard feudalism helped the rebels raise a large number of horsemen. This system meant that soldiers who had originally been recruited for war by contract with the local noble, because the numbers that could be raised by feudalism were inadequate, returned to serve their masters in peace time. In the north it was the custom for the sons of gentry families to serve in the households of the great magnates. This helps explain why the gentry who were involved were often retainers of the two Earls. A study of the supporters shows that many came from the areas around the Neville and Percy households of Brancepeth, Topcliffe and Raby. Feudal allegiance had drawn many into the rising, as those to whom they owed allegiance had joined. However, bastard feudalism was not enough to raise a large enough force and the rebel commanders were forced to resort to religious propaganda, the offer of wages and, in some instances, the threat of force. This was reported to Cecil: 'They have ordered, by force, various people to follow them; the people of Bishopton, tenants of John Conyers, my son-in-law ... they not only forced them to go with them, but compelled the rest of the town, whether they were armed and unarmed, to go to Darlington'. This view that the rebels used force to make others join the rising is supported by an examination of the rebels tried at York in 1570. There, it was discovered that Robert Lambert 'was at the start taken forcefully by the rebels out of his bed, in his father-in-law's house, he had retired there with the intention of going to join Sir George Bowes'. This suggests that rebels were only able to raise their army by threatening people and that popular support was limited.

d) Conclusion

It does appear that it was a combination of political and religious tensions in northern society that triggered the last major threat to the Tudor regime. However, it is harder to decide what was the most important factor. Recent work has argued that resentment towards the growing power and interference of the state played a larger role in the rising than religion; but it must not be forgotten that religion was sufficient to maintain the revolt at Durham for several weeks. A revival of catholic practice still had appeal, and many were willing to destroy the symbols of the new religion.

e) Why did the Rebellion fail?

The very name given to this rising, the Northern Earls' rebellion, may give a clue as to its weakness. It was heavily dependent upon the leadership of the two Earls. This would make it very difficult for them to gather support from areas where they were not well known or lacked supporters. This limited the potential size of any force they could muster. This was to be a vital factor in their defeat. Mary Queen of Scots was being held at Tutbury, Staffordshire; therefore in order to capture her they would have to march through both Lancashire and Cheshire. If they were to win over locals as they made their way south their leadership would need to have popular appeal. However, we have already seen that they did not possess the qualities needed to lead a rebellion, lacking both determination and presence. They certainly did not cut a dash; instead their image is one of reluctant rebels, driven into rebellion out of despair, rather than with an iron will. We have already seen that they had to be pushed into the rising by their wives and this would have hardly given potential supporters confidence to risk life and limb, let alone appeal to locals where their name was scarcely known. Their entry into rebellion also suggests that they did not have a coherent plan and it is hardly surprising that, at the first news of a large royal force, they fled. As a consequence their support was always likely to be limited to the areas where the Earls still had an appeal and they could count on loyalty to the family names. Bastard feudalism had helped gain support in their homelands, but it was a limiting factor as they moved further south. The Earls were not able to draw on support from a wide geographical area and as a result they were able to gather together a force of only 5–6,000 men. And even this force could not be relied upon as some began to desert when they did not receive their pay. Perhaps it should be no surprise that they turned round when they reached Bramham Moor, near York, and headed back northwards to home territory.

The Earls had also hoped for foreign assistance. This may help to explain their actions when retreating. A small force was sent to secure Hartlepool in the hope that Spanish troops would land there. Yet this was unlikely as the Earls had failed to maintain regular contact with any foreign power. It was also improbable that Philip would risk an incursion to help put a pro-French candidate on the English throne. The rebels must have been in a weak and desperate position if they were relying upon Philip. Foreign support for rebels had not been forthcoming in other rebellions, where success had appeared more achievable; it was therefore even less likely this time.

The government also had many advantages. The rebellion was much smaller than the 1536 rising and the government was in a much stronger position in 1569. They already had plans to move Mary further south, probably to Coventry. This would drag the rebels further away from their base of support and draw them into an area where the crown had even more support. Even in the north the monarchy was in a better position than in 1536. The Tudor policy of reducing the autonomy of many of the great families there had started to succeed. Elizabeth's policy of introducing her own men into the north had also begun to pay dividends. The loyalty of men such as Gargrave, who held Pontefract, and Forster, who held Berwick, helped to contain the rising and limit the numbers joining the rebels. Further south it was much easier for the Queen. In both Lancashire and Cheshire she could count on the loyalty of important local figures such as the Bishop of Carlisle and the Earl of Shrewsbury, both of whom were also quite popular with the local catholic communities. However, when Elizabeth did need to raise a force to confront the rebels her task was much easier. The new militia system, whereby the newly appointed Lord Lieutenants, JPs and Commissioners of Muster were required to levy troops, enabled her to raise sufficient numbers that would soon be able to wear down the rising. There were soon rumours abounding that a large royal force was being assembled at Warwick ready to move north. Although the army was slow in moving north the government had been able to raise a force of some 10,000 men. This far outnumbered the rebel force of 6,000 and would have been quite sufficient to defeat them. However, their retreat made this unnecessary.

Religion may have been a significant cause of the revolt, and there can be little doubt that it was a major factor in its failure. Although mass had been restored in a number of churches, religion was no longer a sufficient enough motive to attract large-scale support. The fear of the unknown, which had won mass support for the rebels in 1536, was absent. Inertia was the more common response. Many well-known catholic nobles failed to join the rebellion, realising that they had more to lose than gain in such an incoherent venture. As a consequence the Earls were unable to win support even in areas where there was resistance to protestantism. Catholics probably felt let down. In order to rally support for the rebels the papacy was supposed to issue a decree declaring Elizabeth excommunicated from the Catholic church. This was designed to encourage catholics in both England and the rest of Europe to rise up against her. However, the decree did not arrive until February 22nd 1570, after the rebellion had collapsed. This was typical of the lack of organisation and planning that characterised the rebellion. It is therefore hardly surprising that many catholics were unwilling to risk their lives and fortunes in supporting the scheme. After all, they were scarcely being persecuted and Elizabeth had included as many as possible in local government. Their status and prestige were reasonably secure, but a rebellion might destroy all. The failure of the rebellion of the Northern Earls marked the final settlement of the northern question. Elizabeth was determined to destroy the autonomy of the region once and for all.

4 The Oxfordshire Rising, 1596

KEY ISSUE What can we learn about the powers of the Elizabethan state from the failure of the Oxfordshire Rising?

There had already been a few minor disturbances in the west country in the 1580s due to food shortages, and in the 1590s the government was concerned that there might be a repeat of the 1549 'camping' season (see Chapter 4). The possibility of unrest was not surprising in view of the state of the country. There had been bad harvests, creating food shortages; there was disease; and taxation was high to finance the war with Spain, which had continued since the failed Armada of 1588. However, what is more surprising is the scale of the revolt. The leaders planned to seize the home of the local Lord Lieutenant, take his arms and artillery and march to London. But, despite careful preparation, there assembled only four rebels, who waited for two hours for others to join them. Instead they were arrested and taken to London, where they were examined using torture and executed for levying war against the Queen. Despite the small scale of the rising the Privy Council demanded even more arrests and examinations. Why?

The government was concerned because of the volatile background against which the rising took place. However, it also provided them with the opportunity to demonstrate the powers of the state. It was a clear indication that, even after a decade of starvation, order had triumphed. The state was able to show the scale of force available and use it to discourage other potential troublemakers. Perhaps this lesson had already been learned. An examination of those who were involved shows that they were young unmarried artisans or servants with nothing to lose. Unlike 1549, they were unable to obtain the support of the middling sort who had provided the backbone of Ket's rising. They had also failed to win backing from gentlemen or yeomen – people who now saw that there was more to be gained, in terms of patronage and reward, in supporting the state. As a consequence, the governing and propertied class faced the challenge of rebellion united; any threat from the commons alone would be weak and easily crushed.

5 The Essex Rebellion

> **KEY ISSUES** What were the causes of the Essex Rebellion? Why did it fail?

a) Background

The Earl of Essex had become Elizabeth's favourite courtier. His heroic image gained through fighting duels, and charisma and charm won him many admirers. Although his lofty bearing and aristocratic disposition were legendary, he was short on cash.[6] However, his attempts to rule the court and rival the policies of the Cecils turned the Queen against him. The struggle reached crisis point in July 1598.

During discussion of the appointment of a new Lord Deputy in Ireland Essex opposed Elizabeth's nomination and then turned his back on the Queen. She recalled him, struck him across the face and then dismissed him from court. Striking him before witnesses was a dishonour and Essex felt that he had been done a most serious wrong. His absence from court also meant that he was of little use as a faction leader. He had no access to the Queen and so was unable to obtain rewards and promotion for his supporters. The death of the Queen's Secretary, William Cecil, in August 1598 allowed a reconciliation of sorts to take place between Elizabeth and Essex in October. He had been humbled, but with mounting debts he needed royal support. In March 1599 he appeared to have regained his position as he was appointed Lieutenant in Ireland. However, his future career depended upon success there.

Yet Essex's absence in Ireland gave his enemies the chance to persuade the Queen to fill vacant posts with their supporters. Furthermore military defeats in Ireland weakened his position still further and his conduct of campaigns in Ireland was heavily criticised. In a last desperate attempt to regain influence he left his post without permission in September 1599 and burst unannounced into Elizabeth's bedchamber. It was the end of his career: he was charged with maladministration and abandoning his command. He was suspended from membership of the Privy Council and put under house arrest. Although the sentence was later relaxed, he was still banished from court. Now he was denied that access to the royal presence which he believed was his right as an aristocrat.

In the summer of 1600 the situation became even more serious for Essex as he was charged with treason on the grounds that he had conspired with Spain and the Pope in order to obtain the crown of England. The charges were unfounded, but they were a clear indication that the stakes had risen and that Essex had become increasingly vulnerable. This was made clear in September when the Queen refused to renew his patent for sweet wine. His credit structure collapsed and he was condemned to a life of poverty. Elizabeth refused to give him an audience and his creditors began to arrest his servants who had stood surety. This gave Essex two choices: retire from public life or try to seize power.

b) The Rebellion

As befitted his reputation, Essex decided upon a coup. The plan was to seize Whitehall, where Elizabeth was, and the Tower in order to use it as a military base. Once this had been achieved a parliament would be called, the Privy Council purged and the succession guaranteed to James VI of Scotland. Essex's aims were personal: he wanted to ensure that his position would be secure and gain credit with the new king for his accession and to improve his own position. He also wanted to remove his enemies at court, not the Queen. He believed that power had become concentrated in the hands of one unscrupulous faction who were denying him his rightful place as a dispenser of patronage. However, the plan was suspected and therefore a new scheme was devised to stage a large-scale demonstration in London. But the events of February 8 were a fiasco. Only 300 supporters came to Essex's home. At the same time, four Privy Councillors arrived with a message of conciliation from the Queen, but they were taken hostage. Essex then set off at the head of his small band. They went to the Sheriff's house, where Essex expected to obtain reinforcements, but the Sheriff refused to help and left to defend the City. Meanwhile barricades were erected, reinforcements called and Essex was proclaimed a traitor. Soon he was encircled and had to force his way back to his house. Once there, the government brought artillery from the Tower and Essex surrendered on the condition that he would have a fair trial. The revolt was over. It had lasted a mere 12 hours.

c) Failure

Essex had been unable to raise a sufficient force, as he lacked a power base. Although there were many who disliked the monopoly of influence wielded by the Cecils, they were not an organised group. Only a small number followed Essex into revolt. He was deserted by many of his old friends because they saw that an armed rising was no longer the way to achieve their goals. Essex also lacked the feudal ties that provided earlier aristocratic rebellions with support. He was essentially a courtier, who needed the backing of the Queen, and a military leader, whose strength depended upon captains of the royal army as he did not have personal retainers. As a consequence the rebellion had turned into little more than a riot of young, disaffected and poverty-stricken nobles who had exaggerated the popular support of their leader.

Although the rebellion was the first serious challenge to the regime in the capital for nearly 50 years it had been easily crushed. Essex's failure to win support was an indication of the strength of the Tudor regime. Despite the ageing administration and the concentration of power in the hands of a few, too many had a vested interest in the regime's survival to place their support behind a desperate man. They had too much to lose. The defeat of the rising ensured Robert Cecil's victory, and he was able to issue a list of charges against Essex. Although the accusations – that Essex had sought the Crown, had plotted against the judges and engaged in a catholic conspiracy – were lies, they enabled Cecil to create the atmosphere in which he could ensure the smooth succession of James VI, while he himself would remain as chief minister.

6 Conclusion

The Essex rising had shown that many who might have become entwined in rebellion had been drawn into administration in the counties and were moving away from violence as a means of solving their disputes. They had became drawn into the system of government, and so they worked to reform the behaviour of the lower orders and to contain their potential for riot through measures such as the Elizabethan Poor Law. The gentry had found that there were other ways to express their disapproval of royal policy. This was seen in Elizabeth's last parliament during the ugly debates about the awarding of Monopolies as a means of rewarding courtiers. Rebellion had become the last resort of the isolated and powerless.[7]

The last decade of Elizabeth's reign produced some alarms. The Queen was ageing and losing her political touch and there was intense factional struggle at court. There were battles for power as she refused to name her successor and as her old advisors died and new men sought power. However, despite high taxation, poor harvests, rising prices and disease, the threats were never serious. The Oxfordshire and Essex rebellions were tragi-comic in their lack of success.[8] But there was relief when Elizabeth died and the succession passed safely to James VI. It was a clear indication of how much had been achieved in the period of Tudor rule. Elizabeth had inherited a precarious situation, her half brother and sister had both faced serious challenges, yet the rebellions that she faced were small scale in comparison and never a serious threat to her rule.

References

1 N. Jones, *The Reign of Elizabeth I* ed. C. Haigh (Macmillan, 1984), p. 52.
2 L. Stone, *The Crisis of the Aristocracy* (OUP, 1965), p. 251.
3 C. Sharp, *Memorials of the Rebellion of 1569* (London, 1840), pp. 42–3.
4 A. Fletcher and D. MacCulloch, *Tudor Rebellions* (Longman, 1997), p. 106.
5 C. Sharp, *Memorials*, pp. 42–3.
6 J. Guy, *Tudor England*, p. 439.
7 P. Thomas, *Authority and Disorder in Tudor Times* (CUP, 1999), p. 101.
8 A. Fletcher and D. MacCulloch, *Tudor Rebellions*, p. 112.

Summary Diagram: Elizabeth I
Cause and Membership of the Risings

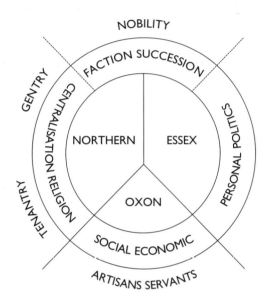

1. Imagery and the Power of the Tudor Monarch
Study carefully the pictures of Elizabeth I on page 83 and Mary Tudor on page 73.

a) What message is the painter trying to convey about the power of Elizabeth and how does he do this? (*10 marks*)

b) Compare the painting of Elizabeth with that of Mary. Which do you consider to be more successful in portraying the power of the Tudor monarch? (*20 marks*)

c) How useful are paintings as sources of evidence about the power of the Tudor monarchy? (*20 marks*)

2. The role of religion in the Northern Rising
Read the comment by the Earl of Westmorland on page 92 and study the picture on page 91.

a) Explain what Westmorland meant when he said 'those who quarrel for that reason in other countries are accounted as rebels'. (*5 marks*)

b) Explain what Westmorland meant when he said that his house was 'a long time preserved without staining'. (*5 marks*)

c) Compare the view of Westmorland with that of the picture. Which source do you think is more reliable? Explain your answer using both details from the sources and your own knowledge about the rising. (*20 marks*)

Answering structured questions on Elizabeth I and the defeat of rebellion.

a) Explain two reasons why there was no crisis when Elizabeth came to the throne. (*30 marks*)

b) Explain two reasons why the situation changed in 1569. (*30 marks*)

c) How far was religion the cause of the Northern Rising of 1569? (*60 marks*)

d) What were the aims of Norfolk and Northumberland in the Northern Rising of 1569? (*30 marks*)

e) To what extent was the Northern Rising the result of the arrival of Mary Queen of Scots in England? (*60 marks*)

7 Conclusion

POINTS TO CONSIDER

This chapter adopts a thematic approach to the rebellions. It draws together some of the major themes that have been raised throughout the earlier chapters This is a very important issue if you are studying unrest for a synoptic or thematic paper and you will need to have a full understanding of the ideas raised. You will need to be able to draw on a wide range of examples from different rebellions, covering the whole period and develop further the ideas raised in this section.

1 The Scale of Rebellion

KEY ISSUE Why were there so many rebellions?

All Tudor monarchs faced the challenge of armed rebellion. It is only the benefit of hindsight that shows us that their rule would be more than temporary. Chapter 1 showed that monarchs lacked forces to control disorder and that they had to rely largely upon informal controls. The weakness of their claim to the throne may also have encouraged challenges in the early period of their rule. If the Tudors could gain the crown by force, what was there to stop others from trying to do the same, or at least improve their political or economic position?

It must also be remembered that riot, violence and affray were commonplace in everyday life. The authorities were always worried about casual violence, particularly food riots and urban unrest. This was a particular worry because of the rapidly changing social and economic situation. The sixteenth century witnessed a population growth that outstripped resources and resulted in a large-scale price rise. As a consequence it was a period of hunger and deprivation, leading to a substantial growth in poverty and vagrancy that the government was unable to control. The lower orders provided an angry and mobile population who would provide the rank and file for riots.

However, if riots were to develop into large-scale rebellion, leadership was vital. The peasantry and mass of those trapped in poverty lacked the capacity and organisational skills necessary to turn local unrest into large-scale challenges to the regime. However, in the first half of the sixteenth century there were those from the middling sections of society who were willing to lead the peasantry. The Pilgrimage of Grace was led by Robert Aske, a successful lawyer, Robert Ket was not just a tanner but also a substantial landowner, whilst Thomas Wyatt had been a member of the English council in France during the reign of Henry VIII.

At the same time, violence was a part of everyday life and this outlook could soon be exploited and turned into rebellion by an ambitious leader or a displaced group. This can be seen in East Anglia when an anti-enclosure riot was used by Ket to settle a local score and became a major rising. Meanwhile groups, such as the clergy, used popular unrest to further their own ends, as was seen in both the Pilgrimage of Grace and the Western Rebellion. Riot was often the only way to draw attention to dissatisfaction with government policies. It was also used by those who felt excluded from their rightful position in society, as was seen in both Wyatt's rebellion and the that of the Northern Earls.

But for many rebellion was the only way, at least in the first half of the sixteenth century, to draw attention to problems. Parliament did not offer the majority of the population the opportunity to air their grievances and challenge the regime; this development occurred only towards the end of the century in the debates on monopolies. For the lower orders, particularly those who suffered from poverty, they had nothing and therefore there was nothing to lose by rebellion.

The sixteenth century witnessed the demise of what was seen as the 'natural order'. The traditional ruling aristocracy was often replaced by new men from the rising class of lawyers. This was disconcerting for a society that believed in a hierarchical structure. There were fears that the traditional balance was being turned upside down with the emergence of low-born councillors, such as Wolsey and Cromwell. Even Elizabeth recruited councillors from outside the traditional aristocratic circle and it appeared to nobles, such as Northumberland, Westmorland and Essex, that their predominance was at an end. Their traditional role as rulers was being lost and their prestige and status were declining. As with the lower orders, so with the excluded nobility: they had little to lose by rebellion and believed that they might be able to recover the influence and favour they considered their birth demanded.

The religious changes of the mid-Tudor period also played a crucial role in causing unrest. The religious upheavals, particularly between 1534 and 1559, were a direct cause of the Pilgrimage of Grace, the Western Rebellion and Northern Rebellion. However, the Reformation also destroyed confidence in the church, and there was no longer a comforting set of rituals that enforced basic social discipline. As a result many people lost confidence in the church and its role as an upholder of authority. Many of the changes, particularly events such as the Dissolution, were unpopular. Destroying a way of life and beliefs that had been accepted for centuries, they resulted in social and religious changes that loosened the bonds that had helped to bind society together. The priests lost their role as arbiters of the community's morals, leaving individuals without guidance. Religious change helped to destroy traditional concepts of authority at both a local and central level.

The inability of governments to deal with unrest allowed riots to develop into something more threatening. As the Tudors lacked a standing army to deal with unrest, they relied upon the local leaders of society to nip trouble in the bud. However, this did not always happen. In both the Western Rebellion and Ket's the absence of resident gentry allowed minor disturbances to escalate. Meanwhile, in the case of the Pilgrimage of Grace, the failure of the local nobility to support the regime allowed the rising to grow and seize strategic strongholds that allowed the rebels to threaten the security of the realm. This lack of control was a particular problem for the monarchy in the more peripheral areas, where nobles behaved like 'kings' and the rule of the crown was enforced more in theory than practice.

2 The Causes of Rebellion

KEY ISSUE Did the rebellions have anything in common?

The economic problems, the religious changes of the Reformation and the dynastic problems of the Tudors all resulted in breakdowns in law and order. The ensuing revolts took a variety of forms, but historians have identified two broad categories of rebellion. The first were simple protests, or demonstrations, where the aim of the rebels was to achieve a redress of their grievances, or at least to draw the government's attention to their problems and difficulties. The second type of rebellion was concerned with trying to either seize political power by presenting their own alternative for the throne, or to achieve a better and more powerful position for themselves in the running of the country.

a) Protests and Demonstrations

Many of the rebellions asked for the redress of grievances. Sometimes they were confined to one specific problem, but in most cases there was a wide range of issues. The most common cause of complaint was probably taxation. Increasing tax demands, particularly when prices were rising, put an ever-growing pressure on the peasantry who lacked the means to increase their incomes to meet such exactions. The growing power of the state and the demands of war were the major cause of the increasing fiscal pressures, and this was seen in the Cornish Rising of 1497 and the Taxation Rebellion of 1524. Even the rumour of taxation was often enough to spark rebellion, particularly if it came in the wake of poor harvests or a worsening economic climate. This was certainly the case in both the Lincolnshire Rising and the Pilgrimage of Grace.

The majority of the population was faced by a deteriorating economic situation. There were rising prices, population growth and poverty and vagrancy, any of which was sufficient to spark unrest. These social grievances played a major role in many of the rebellions, particularly those of 1549. However, we must be careful when assessing the role of economic factors because much of the sixteenth century was a period of distress and it is therefore possible to argue that there should have been unrest every year, particularly in the 1590s when the situation was at its worst. In light of this, it is probably fair to suggest that although economic factors were important they were not the primary cause of rebellion. They became important when pressures were too great, usually at times of war when demands for taxation rose, when enclosure denied the peasantry their common lands, or during periods of particularly rapid price and trade variations.

Most rebellions that were concerned with the redress of grievance also had other factors in common. Although it may not always appear obvious, the rebels were fundamentally loyal, frequently claiming that they supported the state. In the 1540s the rebels claimed that they were supporters of the government's social policy against greedy landlords who were exploiting them. The rebels believed that the government supported them as they struggled to bring recalcitrant gentry into line. Leaders, such as Ket, argued that they were representing the king against men who should have been keeping order and justice, but were failing to carry out their duty. The rebels resorted to violence and pulled down hedges because it was the only way they could right a wrong once the gentry had refused to carry out their obligations. Direct action was commonplace in these disturbances because the commons wanted results, not revolution.

The idea that these rebels were more obedient than they seemed is illustrated by an examination of the nature of their demands and their behaviour. The Pilgrim oath makes it very clear that their aim is 'only for the love that you do bear unto Almighty God his faith, and the Holy Church militant and its maintenance' and 'the preservation of the King's person'.[1] This deference is continued when the Pilgrims, despite their vastly superior numbers, made no attempt to bring the royal forces to battle and dispersed when promised that their grievances would be listened to. The same behaviour was seen in Ket's rebellion: when the rebels issued their demands they were all prefaced with the phrase 'We pray your Grace'. In both Ket's rebellion and the Pilgrimage the leaders took steps to ensure that the rank and file behaved in an orderly manner. Despite the large forces available to both Ket and Aske, there is no evidence of theft and pillage, or serious attacks on the gentry. Ket issued ordinances for the collection of supplies, and even these were in the same form as government warrants. The leadership had made it very clear that they supported the government and did not want to see anarchy.

The religious changes of the mid-sixteenth century also played a significant role in provoking unrest. In these instances the rebels usually aimed at the reversal of the government's religious policy. An examination of the demands shows that all the religiously motivated rebellions aimed at reversing the apparent moves towards protestantism and demanding a return to the old ways. In both the Pilgrimage and the Western Rebellion, they claimed that they were acting in a legitimate fashion. The Pilgrims argued that Henry had been misadvised as the Lords had failed to tell him of the importance of the monasteries in the north. Meanwhile, the Western rebels claimed that the government did not have the authority to make religious changes until Edward was 24. However, the Western Rebels expressed themselves in a more aggressive manner than the Pilgrims, starting their grievances with 'We will have'.

The large numbers that both rebellions attracted also suggests that there was a genuine feeling that the rebels were undertaking a legitimate form of action and that they were gathering for a proper purpose.

However, there were differences between the Pilgrimage and the Western Rebellion. The Pilgrimage was a much more orderly affair, where the rebels obeyed the leadership and dispersed when they believed that their grievances would be listened to. They certainly had justification to claim that they were obedient subjects. This contrasted sharply with the Western Rebels who were much more obdurate and rebellious, forcing government forces into at least five skirmishes or serious encounters. The rebels were also more violent in their behaviour and wanted to kill the local gentry.

The Northern Rebellion of 1569 used to be seen as a religious rising. It had similarities with the Pilgrimage, insofar as the rebels tried to make the rising legitimate by claiming to act in the Queen's name, in the true interests of the realm and out of a duty to God. However, unlike the Pilgrims they were not concerned if their demands were legitimate and were more willing to act in a treasonous manner to achieve their ends. Recent research has shown that the rising was not just about religion, but also about politics and the succession, and for this reason it has more in common with the second category of risings.

b) The Overthrow of the Regime

It is true to say that nearly all the rebellions covered in this book either put forward alternative claimants to the throne or intended to determine the succession. This was due, at least in part, to the dynastic uncertainties of the period, and was particularly true under Henry VII, when his hold on the crown was tenuous. However, this theme continued right through the period. Both Perkin Warbeck and Lambert Simnel attempted to alter the succession and improve the position of the Yorkists who had lost out following Richard's defeat at Bosworth. The Pilgrimage of Grace wanted Mary restored to the succession, whilst Mary Tudor's campaign against the Lady Jane Grey affair was an attempt to restore the legitimate ruler. Wyatt's rebellion, despite the claims that he raised forces in the name of the queen and for her protection and preservation against foreigners, was an attempt to depose Mary and install Elizabeth. The rebellion was against the monarch, even though they dare not admit it, even to their followers. The Northern Rebellion aimed to determine the succession to the throne, and possibly overthrow the monarch. In order to give the rising the appearance of legitimacy, the rebels needed to capture Mary Queen of Scots, and it can be argued that it was for this reason that the government moved her further south from Tutbury. The lack of numbers involved in the rising, perhaps 6,000, also suggests that it was an aristocratic conspiracy not about religion or economic problems, but the succession and power in the north.

Many of those involved in these more drastic and treasonous rebellions were from either the aristocracy or gentry. They included men such as Thomas Wyatt, the Earls of Northumberland, Westmorland and Essex. These were all men who had lost their influence with the monarch and were involved in a last desperate attempt to regain their former status. This was certainly true of those mentioned above and was also the situation facing both the Aragonese faction who were involved in the Pilgrimage of 1536 and the Duke of Northumberland in his attempted coup of 1553. However, it is also noticeable that, apart from the Pilgrimage of Grace, the rebellions that aimed at altering the succession, such as Wyatt's or Northumberland's, or those that aimed at changing the monarch's advisors, such as Essex, attracted the least amount of support. It is perhaps this factor that helps us to answer our next question.

3 The failure of Rebellion

KEY ISSUE Why were most rebellions unsuccessful?

Despite the limited forces available to the early-modern state, most Tudor rebellions ended in failure and defeat. In most instances the rebels were defeated, often with very heavy casualties, on the battlefield, or dispersed with empty promises that were not kept. However, this view is simplistic: it assumes that their aim was a military victory and the overthrow of the regime, rather than a demonstration. In many instances the rebels did not want to topple the regime, but to bring their grievances to the attention of the government, and therefore simply raising a rebellion was a triumph in itself. Only when the aim was to overthrow the regime and replace the reigning monarch is it possible to argue convincingly that the rebellion was a failure.

However, if we do believe that Tudor rebellions did ultimately fail, what arguments can be put forward to explain that failure? Many rebellions met their demise on the battlefield. Despite the lack of a standing or professional army, the state could, given time, gather together a sufficient force to defeat untrained rebel forces. The government's tactic of playing for time and negotiating with the rebels, with offers of pardon, allowed them the opportunity to assemble a well-equipped and trained force that could wreak havoc on a battlefield. This was seen to great effect at Stoke, Dussindale and Clyst Heath. Stories of such slaughter may also have discouraged potential rebels in the future. Even when the rebels appeared to have an advantage they did not seem able to seize it, perhaps unable to comprehend their success and unsure what to do next.

This was largely due to the nature of the protests, which were often local in their aims. Ket's rebellion wanted to bring about reform to local government in East Anglia, whilst the Cornish Rebellion was concerned about the inequality of taxation in the west of the kingdom. This limited the appeal of the grievances and prevented the rebels from seeking help from outside the area. As the rebels' aims were often local, it is hardly surprising that they attempted to seize the regional capital. Although some rebellions succeeded – so that Ket took Norwich, the Pilgrims York and the Northern Earls Durham – the rebels needed to take London, the national capital, if they were to bring about the defeat of the government. However, London was a long way from the source of the unrest; and, as many of the grievances were local, the commons, which made up the rank and file of the rebel force, had no desire to leave their locality. When rebel forces did move away from the source, numbers declined as the peasantry returned home, concerned about their crops and harvest or worried about journeying into an unknown region. The result was that the rebel force was often small by the time it had left its local area. In response to this problem the leaders of both Ket's rebellion and the Western kept the rebels in the local area, diminishing their threat to central government. Therefore, although the challenges tended to come from the peripheral areas of the kingdom, where the royal writ was less strong, this fact had the advantage of giving the government time to assemble an army to challenge the rebels before they reached the capital.

Most rebel armies lacked the numerical strength to challenge the monarchy as many inhabitants were unwilling to become involved in unrest. They wanted nothing more than to be able to live a quiet life and did not have the time to abandon their precarious existence for a cause they probably did not understand. In the Northern Rebellion only 6,000 took part, despite the popularity of the religious complaints, and often those who did take part had to be forced or bribed to do so. The population may also have been more law-abiding, giving greater support to legitimate rule, than was once thought. The rebellions that challenged the Tudor right to rule failed to attract significant numbers. Wyatt's rebellion showed how difficult it was to raise a force against the crown. He could assemble a force of only 2,000, despite remaining silent about deposing Mary and installing Elizabeth on the throne. In order to increase the size of his force Wyatt tried to avoid admitting they were rebels against the Queen, even to his supporters. However, the most treasonous revolt of the period attracted little support from the common people, despite the unpopularity of Mary's marriage, and Wyatt's attempt was defeated in two weeks.[2] On the other hand, the common people rallied to Mary, a year earlier, in order to ensure that the legitimate ruler did gain the throne and Northumberland's attempted coup failed.

In many of the risings the rebels counted upon foreign support. Yet the small level of support that was forthcoming from abroad may also help to explain the failure of the rebellions. Nearly all the challenges to Henry VII had overseas help, but their foreign backers were not prepared to supply a large number of troops or vast funds. This suggests that they were aware that the enterprise was probably doomed to failure and they were not prepared to risk losing soldiers or a large fortune for little gain. Instead they settled for being of nuisance value to Henry and prevented him from feeling completely secure. Later in the period foreign help failed to materialise at all; this was true during the Pilgrimage of Grace and the Northern Rebellion. Once again foreign rulers may have realised the futility of the cause and saw little to be gained from it. This failure to obtain overseas help made it much easier for the government as they did not have to deal with the threat of invasion, on top of the problem of the rising.

However, it would be wrong to dismiss all rebellions of the period as a failure and they need to be judged against their aims. The Tudors had gained the throne by an armed rising and this might be considered the first successful Tudor rebellion. Perhaps most surprisingly, it can be argued that it was the strongest of the Tudor kings, Henry VIII, who suffered the greatest defeats at the hands of rebels. The Amicable Grant of 1525 was first halved, as the king blamed Wolsey for its severity, then abandoned completely and no money came in. We have already seen in Chapter 3 that the Pilgrimage of Grace succeeded in assembling a large proportion of all the able-bodied men from the north and delayed the implementation of further religious changes. When the Pilgrims were promised concessions they tore off their badges and went home. It is interesting to speculate what Henry would have done about the promises he had made if the Cumberland Rising of 1537 had not given him the excuse he needed to exact revenge.

But perhaps the greatest success for any armed rising was in 1553. The government was in the hands of Northumberland, and his daughter-in-law, Lady Jane Grey, was queen. He controlled the Tower, Council and the Exchequer and was well defended by military men. Northumberland appeared to be in a strong position and able to prevent Henry's next heir from taking her rightful inheritance. Yet by standing firm and claiming to be the legitimate ruler, Mary was able to attract large numbers to her cause and take the throne without an armed struggle. However, she was fortunate a year later. Although Wyatt was defeated it can be argued that his rebellion was a close-run thing and that it did have a significant impact on the long-term development of the Tudor state. Wyatt's rebellion had shown how unpopular the marriage to Philip II was, and it is possible to argue that it was this that prompted the Spanish king to remain out of England for long periods. If this is true, it had a major impact on the succession as his absence ensured that there was no catholic heir to succeed. This, rather ironically, gave Wyatt long-term success as he had helped to ensure that it was Elizabeth and protestantism that triumphed, even if it had to wait until 1558.

4 The decline of rebellion

KEY ISSUE Why did the threat of rebellion diminish?

When the rebellion of the Northern Earls was defeated no one was to know that it would be the last major challenge to the Tudor regime. Although 1569 did not mark the end of unrest the later challenges were small-scale, shot-lived and local. The challenge of Essex was no more than that of a factious magnate, whilst the Oxfordshire rising scarcely deserves its name. There were still enclosure riots, but they did not develop into serious revolts as had happened in 1549. It appeared as if the dangers of 1549 had shown the ruling classes that popular disturbance and religious dissent were too dangerous to tolerate.

There was certainly a change in attitude among the ruling elite towards rebellion. The near anarchy of 1549 marked a turning point in the outlook of the nobles. Before then they had led the challenges to the regime and it was from them that nearly all crises had stemmed. However, in the second half of the century, there was a reformation in manners among the gentry and aristocracy as an ideology of order and obedience developed. There was less use of threats and violence to right wrongs and a greater use of litigation. By the end of the century the rate of popular litigation at the central courts per head of the population was higher than ever before. As the behaviour of the ruling class improved, so they tried to improve that of the lower orders. The gentry were more willing to squash rebellious enthusiasm and unrest among the lower orders.

The ruling class had also found other ways to express their displeasure at government policies. They preferred to use parliament to voice their discontent, as was seen in the Monopolies debates at the end of Elizabeth's reign. At the same time, these men who, in the past, had provided the leadership for most of the risings had been drawn into an alliance with central government. As a result they identified themselves more closely with the state, rather than the commons. Growing educational opportunities meant that the landowning class had been able to educate itself for public office and would now close ranks against the lower born.[3] The gentry had become more closely involved in county and shire administration, acting as JPs, Lord Lieutenants and Provost Marshals. This gave them prestige and status among their fellow men and they were not willing to lose their good name or property by becoming involved in rebellion.

These developments had resulted in a growing polarisation between the rich and the poor. The prosperous traders and landowners looked to the ruling class for protection and an alliance developed between the gentry and the middling sort. This is also seen in architectural, cultural and intellectual developments as the rich distanced themselves from the lower class. Two examples show this trend. The first is in architecture, where the wealthy wanted greater privacy, and so servants no longer ate in the great hall and had their own back stairs. The second example is in social policy. The state gradually took on greater responsibility for the welfare of the poor, removing the link and obligation that the middling sort had towards the lower orders.

This development also illustrates two other reasons for the decline in unrest. Tudor governments always feared the threat that could come from the poor and vagrants. However, as the state took on greater social powers, so it was able to bring the problem of poverty under control. This was evident in the 1590s when, despite dearth, there was no serious challenge to the regime. Perhaps central government had learnt from the civic authorities in Exeter who, in 1549, had managed to keep the city loyal to the crown by ensuring that the poor were provided with food and wood. At the same time, the government also had draconian powers available with which to discipline the poor, and Elizabeth was always willing to use them as a warning and example. The power of the state had grown during the sixteenth century and this made it much easier for the government to deal with unrest. Elizabeth had created a larger government machine, with offices such as Lord Lieutenant, and this increased control over village life and prevented minor riots from escalating. This was most evident in the Oxfordshire Rising and may help to explain why it failed to materialise. But it also showed the increased power of the state and its ability to make examples, as those involved were soon taken to London to be interrogated and then executed. The state arm reached a lot further at the end of the period than at the beginning.

Elizabeth also had the backing of the church to help bolster the regime. Although it had lost much authority and respect during the Reformation it had regained its position by the end of the century as another arm of the state. The protestant religion appealed more to the educated gentry, and as a result an alliance between them and the clergy gradually developed. The clergy started to distance themselves from their ordinary parishioners and began to copy the life-style of the more prosperous in society. They preached obedience, and as a result the pulpit became one of the most important vehicles of social and political control. However, at the same time the rise of household puritansim also helped impose discipline as it also taught the values of obedience and order.

The start of Elizabeth's reign had brought hope to those who had been excluded under previous rulers. Elizabeth was able to exploit this and the growing prejudice in favour of the Tudors, particularly when many of the challenges came from her religious opponents, often with foreign support. She knew how to gratify and manage her nobility, and it was not until the final years that serious creaks in the system were obvious, as Essex's challenge showed. However, as his rising also showed, rebellion was now the last resort of desperate men. For the ruling class there was too much to be lost. The population was also more willing to conform to the requirements of public order, encouraged by reminders from the pulpit and proclamations. The ruling class was more cohesive in administering the shires and in dealing with unrest. Rapid religious change was a thing of the past, and dynastic uncertainty had been largely resolved in most people's minds.

References

1 Letters and Papers of Henry VIII, xi, 705.
2 A. Wall, *Power and Protest*, pp. 178–9.
3 P. Williams, *The Later Tudors*, pp. 151–2.

Summary Diagram: Conclusion – Classifying Rebellions

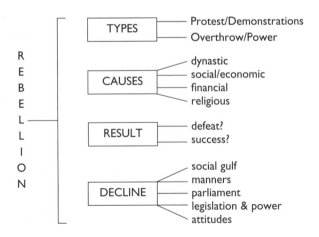

Answering essay questions on Chapter 7

One of the features of the new A level specifications has been the introduction of the synoptic element. This requires the study of a theme over a period of about 100 years. The unrest of the Tudor period provides an ideal topic and has been adopted by some of the examination boards. This requires you to have an overall view of the rebellions throughout the period, be able to compare them and see themes running through the whole period. The questions that are set are broader than the traditional A level essay, but still require the same type of analytical approach. It will also be vital that you draw your examples from the whole period that you have studied. The following give you some idea of the types of questions that can be set:

a) How seriously challenged was the Tudor regime by rebellions and unrest?

b) Which rebellion presented the greatest challenge to the Tudor monarchy?

c) Why did Tudor rebellions fail?

d) To what extent was religion the main cause of rebellion in the Tudor period?

e) Why did the Tudor regime experience so many rebellions?

f) Why did the threat of rebellion decline during the Tudor period?

Answers to question (b) could simply go through each rebellion and analyse or describe its threat to the regime. However, better answers will take a thematic approach and also raise the issue of what is meant by 'challenge'. This approach will also prevent you from simply telling the story of each rebellion. You will also find that you have a great deal of information available for such essays and you will need to ensure that you focus on the question set – be relevant! At the end of each paragraph you should try and reach a conclusion about the issue considered as this will help to keep you focused on the question. These conclusions will also serve as the basis for the overall conclusion. The following might serve as a skeleton plan.

- Introduction: Outline the ways in which you can judge the threat presented by a rebellion.
- Paragraph one: Examine the achievements of rebellions, the success of the rebellion against the Amicable Grant, the success of the Pilgrims, the success of Wyatt.
- Paragraph two: Consider the numbers involved. The possibility of foreign help.
- Paragraph three: The force taken, and battles needed, to put down the revolts.
- Paragraph four: The areas controlled by the rebels.
- Paragraph five: The demands made by the rebels, were they challenging the monarchy?

- Paragraph six: The security of the monarch at the time. Was Henry VII more secure in 1485–7 than the rule of a minor in 1549 or a woman in 1554?
- Conclusion: Sum up the main points from each paragraph. Show how reaching an overall conclusion depends upon the different criteria used.

In order to help prepare for question such as (d) it might be helpful to draw up a summary chart showing the different causes of each rebellion. The headings might include religion, economic and social, dynastic, financial and local.

Further Reading

1 General

There are many books available that survey the whole of the Tudor period. The best of the recent publications is probably **John Guy**, *Tudor England* (Oxford, 1998) and this is now available in paperback. *The Tudor Years* edited by **John Lotherington** (Hodder, 1994) is a valuable textbook and ideal in providing the reader with the context for the rebellions. Along the same lines, and ideal as a bridge between GCSE and AS, is *The Tudor Century, 1485–1603* by **Ian Dawson** (Nelson, 1993). Those students who are looking to develop their understanding of the period as a whole should try to read something by **Geoffrey Elton**, either *Reform and Reformation* (London, 1977), or *England under the Tudors* (London, 1955).

2 Rebellion and Order

The best study of Tudor Rebellions is still *Tudor Rebellions* (Longman, 1968) by **Anthony Fletcher**, but now revised by **Diarmaid MacCulloch**. However, this does not cover the reign of Henry VII and is very superficial in its treatment of the later years of Elizabeth. The collection of documents is still very useful. There are a number of books containing collections of essays on particular aspects of rebellions or on specific rebellions. Among the best are *Order and Disorder in Early Modern England* (Cambridge, 1985), edited by **Fletcher** and **Stevenson**, in particular the essay on the Pilgrimage of Grace is a must for A level students, and *Rebellion, Popular Protest and Social Order in Early Modern England* (Cambridge, 1984), edited by **Paul Slack**. The latter contains useful essays on the Pilgrimage and Ket's rebellion. Of the more recent general works on order and disorder, **Alison Wall's** *Power and Protest in England 1525–1640* (Arnold, 2000) introduces the forces available for keeping law and order.

3 Individual Rebellions

a) Lambert Simnel and Perkin Warbeck

There have been few individual studies of these rebellions and readers will need to turn to the more general histories of Henry VII. The most authoritative is still **S.B. Chrimes**, *Henry VII* (Methuen, 1972). Simnel is covered by **M.J. Bennett**, *Lambert Simnel and the Battle of Stoke* (Gloucester, 1987) and Warbeck and the 1497 conspiracy by **I. Arthurson** in his two studies, *The Perkin Warbeck Conspiracy, 1491–1499* (Stroud, 1994) and 'The Rising of 1497: A Revolt of the Peasantry?' in *People, Politics and Community in the Later Middle Ages* ed. **Rosenthal** and **Richmond** (Stroud, 1987). However, in order to see the risings in the wider context, you should consult **Christine Carpenter**, *The Wars of the Roses* (Cambridge, 1997). Foreign influence was also important and it is worth looking at the relevant chapters in **R.B. Wernham**, *Before the Armada: The growth of English Foreign Policy, 1485–1588* (Cape, 1966).

b) The Yorkshire and Cornish Rebellions

There is little readily available without reference to specific journals such as *Northern History* or the *English Historical Review*.

c) Resistance to Taxation

There are few individual studies of this, but the most comprehensive treatment is by **G.W. Bernard** in *War, Taxation and Rebellion in Early Tudor England* (Harvester, 1986).

d) The Lincolnshire Rising and the Pilgrimage of Grace

The comprehensive study of the Pilgrimage was written by the **Dodds**, *The Pilgrimage of Grace and the Exeter Conspiracy* (Cambridge, 1915), but of the recent work candidates should try and read at least the introduction and conclusion of **Michael Bush's** *The Pilgrimage of Grace* (Manchester, 1996). This is a very detailed study of the rebel armies. Candidates might also refer to **R.W. Hoyle's** *The Pilgrimage of Grace* (OUP, 2001), who argues that the rising was the work of the commons, particularly the artisans. It is also worth reading the relevant chapter in *Resistance and Reformation in Tudor Lancashire* (Cambridge, 1975) by **Christopher Haigh**.

e) The 1549 Rebellions

There are a number of studies of both Ket's and the Western Rebellion. The most accessible on Ket's rebellion are probably by **Stephen Land**, *Kett's Rebellion* (Boydell, 1977) and **Julian Cornwall's** *Revolt of the Peasantry 1549* (Routledge and Kegan Paul, 1977). Books on the Western rebellion are limited. There is coverage by **Julian Cornwall** in *The Revolt of the Peasantry*, but otherwise it is the classic study by **Rose-Troup**, *The Western Rebellion of 1549* (Smith, Elder, 1913). All the rebellions of 1549 are considered by **Barrett L. Beer** in *Rebellion and Riot: Popular Disorder in England during the Reign of Edward VI* (Kent, Ohio, 1982).

f) Wyatt's Rebellion

The best study of Wyatt's rebellion is still **David Loades**, *Two Tudor Conspiracies* (Cambridge, 1965).

g) The Revolt of the Northern Earls

There is little readily available on the Northern Rebellion. Perhaps the most useful is **D. Marcombe**, 'A rude and heady people: the local community and the rebellion of the northern Earls' in *The Last Principality, Religion and Society in the Bishopric of Durham, 1494–1660*, ed. **D. Marcombe** (University of Nottingham, 1987). However, there are biographies of the leading protagonists, such as **N. Williams**, *Thomas Howard, Fourth Duke of Norfolk* (Rockcliff, 1964).

h) Elizabeth's Last Years

The best general survey of unrest at the end of the period is **D.E. Underdown's** *Revel, riot and rebellion: Popular politics and culture In England, 1603–1660* (Oxford, 1985). A more detailed study of Essex's rebellion can be found in **M. James** 'At a Cross-roads of the Political Culture: the Essex Revolt, 1601' in *The World of the Favourite,* edited by **J.H. Elliott** and **L.W. B. Brockliss** (New Haven and London, 1999).

Articles

The Tudor period is less well served by A level journals than the Modern period. However, students should consult back copies of *History Review.* There have been a series of articles on most of the Tudor monarchs and these place the rebellions in the wider context of the reign. There is a useful article on the impact of the Pilgrimage of Grace in *History Review,* September 2000. There have been a series of good articles on a variety of rebellions in *Past and Present.* For instance, **M. E. James**, 'The Lincolnshire Rebellion 1536' in *Past and Present* no. 48 and **D. MacCulloch** 'Kett's Rebellion in Context' in no. 84.

Index